Dr James W Anderson is Professor of Medicine and Clinical Nutrition at the University of Kentucky in Lexington. For the past twenty years he has specialized in the treatment of diabetes as well as maintaining a busy medical practice. His research team at the University of Kentucky has developed and tested the new high carbohydrate and fibre (HCF) diets which help diabetic patients to control their condition. Currently Dr Anderson directs the Diabetes Service at the Veterans Administration Medical Centre, where he has an active research and teaching programme.

Dr Anderson is author of the very successful book – *Diabetes – A practical new guide to healthy living* – also in the Positive Health Guide series.

He is married and the father to two children. The Anderson family enjoy travelling together. Dr Anderson believes in regular exercise, which he takes by jogging and playing tennis. He also collects stamps.

OPTIMA

DR ANDERSON'S
HCF DIET

*The new high-fibre, low-cholesterol way
to keep slim and healthy*

Dr James W Anderson

POSITIVE HEALTH GUIDE

To Gay, Kathy and Steve with love

© James W. Anderson 1984

First published in the United Kingdom in 1984 by
Martin Dunitz Limited, London

Reprinted 1985
This edition published in 1990 by
Macdonald Optima, a division of
Macdonald & Co. (Publishers) Ltd

A member of Maxwell Macmillan Pergamon Publishing Corporation

British Library Cataloguing in Publication Data
Anderson, James W.
    Dr Anderson's HCF diet.—(Positive health guide)
    1. Cookery   2. Food—Carbohydrate content
    3. Food—Fiber content
    I. Title   II. Series
    641.5'638   TX652
ISBN 0 356 14480 1

Macdonald & Co. (Publishers) Ltd
Orbit House
1 New Fetter Lane
London EC4A IAR

Phototypeset in Garamond by Book Ens, Saffron Walden, Essex

Printed by Toppan Printing Company (S) Pte Ltd, Singapore

> *Royalties from the book
> will be donated
> towards nutrition
> research*

Front cover photograph shows: *Frozen fresh fruit salad (top, see page 112),
Oat spice biscuits (centre right, see page 45), Stuffed peppers (centre left, see
page 70), Cashew chicken (bottom, see page 102)*

CONTENTS

INTRODUCTION

We are what we eat: in the eighteenth century the French chef and writer Brillat-Savarin said, 'Show me what you eat and I'll tell you who you are.' Now people are becoming more and more conscious of the need to eat the right foods to stay healthy. Packaged and processed foods contain fats and substances that eaten regularly in large amounts can contribute to heart disease and high blood pressure. Changing to the HCF diet will improve your health and well-being and, unlike so many quick reducing diets, will help you lose weight permanently if you need to.

The letters HCF stand for high carbohydrate and fibre, and the diet recommends more of these foods, so reducing the fat, sugar and salt intake. We stress the use of fresh, unprocessed foods: whole-grain cereal such as oats, barley and whole wheat; fresh garden vegetables and fruit; the pulses such as kidney beans, haricot beans and lentils; and eating low-fat dairy products, poultry, fish and lean meat.

What's new about the HCF diet?

Fibre has been the key word in health and fitness diets for more than five years and many previous diet plans and recipe books have focused on whole-wheat bran. So what is there about the HCF diet that makes it better than the others? We have found that there are two different types of fibre and the important point about the HCF diet is that it gives you adequate amounts of both: insoluble, found in wheat bran and soluble, in oats and legumes (beans).

You need the insoluble fibre for a regular bowel movement. The insoluble fibre, or roughage, promotes growth of bacteria in the intestine that make a soft, bulky stool. Efficient working of the intestines prevents many diseases of the gut: varicose veins, diverticular disease and haemorrhoids, all common in the Western world, are less frequent among people with high-fibre intakes and regular bowel movements.

The water-soluble or gummy fibre of oats and beans helps in a different way. It acts on the sugar and fats in the blood, preventing accumulation and so reducing the danger of clotting and narrowed arteries. By smoothing the sugar and helping the body burn it, water-soluble fibre also reduces people's chances of developing diabetes.

The high-carbohydrate part of the diet is useful in another way too. Together, cereals and pulses provide protein-rich, economical and satisfying nutrition that is low in fat, calories and salt. For this reason we recommend a high proportion in the diet. Cooked correctly and combined with fresh foods and interesting flavours, they make a very attractive meal – as the recipes in the book will show you.

Foods to avoid on the HCF diet
Along with the increased intake of both types of fibre there are the 'bad guys' to be avoided:

● **Sugar** in any of its highly concentrated forms is one of the gremlins or bad guys we try to avoid. Stay away from foods that have lots of sugar, fructose or honey added.

● **Fat** is the second gremlin that we limit on the diet. Visible fats, as in lard or butter, as well as invisible fats, as in nuts, both provide 9 calories per gram, or twice the calories of starches or proteins. Unnoticed fat slips extra calories into your diet and adversely affects your health. Fat intake contributes to heart disease, certain forms of cancer, obesity, high blood pressure, diabetes and hardening of the arteries. Thus, reducing your intake of all forms of fat is one of your best health and life insurance buys.

● **Salt** is the third gremlin that we monitor. Although our body requires only a dash of salt a day, most of us eat several teaspoons. Reducing your salt intake lessens your likelihood of developing high blood pressure.

But the HCF diet is not a long list of 'don'ts' and 'no nos'. The meal plans and recipes direct you to a very enjoyable variety of foods that are guaranteed to stimulate your palate.

How was the HCF diet developed?
In Lexington, Kentucky we run diabetes and heart clinics where we do a lot of research on ways of controlling our patients' conditions by diet rather than medication. In 1974 we noted the advantages of fibre in smoothing out our patients' blood sugar and, looking into different types, we discovered this basic difference between the soluble and insoluble fibres.

During the last ten years that we have studied the HCF diet, we have also shown that the soluble or gummy fibre in oats and beans acts directly to lower the blood cholesterol (see page 10). The best sources are oat bran, the branny outer coat of the oat groat produced during the milling of oat flour, and beans. They have more than twice as much soluble or gummy fibre as rolled oats or oatmeal. When we include 75 g/3 oz of either oat bran or beans in the diet of people with cholesterol problems, their blood cholesterol drops by 20 per cent or 60 mg/100 ml. When they continue to use oat bran or beans at home – eating, say, three oat bran muffins or porridge plus beans every day – their blood cholesterol remains at these lower levels.

Another exciting discovery has been that the HCF diet lowers blood pressure by about 10 per cent. In addition to reducing clogging of the arteries, fibre has a definite effect on blood pressure (see page 12). We are still doing research on the best programme for treating high blood pressure with diet.

So, with these careful research studies we have been able to collect accurate information on how the HCF diet works and its benefits.

Who should use the HCF diet?

After ten years of research and testing we are able to say definitely that the diet will offer additional benefits to adults and children already enjoying good health. Recently, several national governments have made dietary recommendations for the whole population. All of them recommended eating more foods with starch and fibre, fewer foods with fat and cholesterol, and reductions in the use of sugar and salt. Even if you consider yourself fit and healthy, when you look at the types of food you eat you may be surprised at their high fat and sugar content – these are storing up trouble for the future.

No nutrition plan can guarantee health and well-being. Your environment, heredity, lifestyle and personality traits also affect your health. Keys to health include diet, exercise, relaxation and moderation. But the HCF diet provides the framework to develop healthy eating patterns and, in the long run, lose weight.

On average 30 per cent of the population living in Western countries are overweight. The HCF diet is a good choice if you want to lose weight. High-fibre foods take longer to eat than other types, leaving you feeling more satisfied. Eating three apples requires about fifteen minutes, while getting the same calories from apple juice takes only one and a half minutes. High-fibre foods are more filling than low-fibre ones. Several careful scientific studies show that the sense of fullness is much greater after fibre-rich meals than after low-fibre ones, and since they are more nutritious too you don't get as hungry between meals. High-fibre foods also provide fewer calories than do similar low-fibre foods (see the table overleaf). Some starch is not digested so that on the HCF diet you lose more calories with the bowel movements than with a conventional diet. All of these factors enable you to lose weight without depriving yourself of a variety of delicious foods.

Anyone who is in good health can begin the HCF diet straightaway. The meal plans and recipes in this book show you how to follow a fully nutritious and varied diet, and if you want to reduce your weight, the calorie values given with the recipes will help you do this easily.

People with some of the conditions I describe below should talk to their doctor before going on the diet: anyone who is under medical supervision should as a matter of course consult the doctor before altering the daily routine in any way.

High-fibre foods	Low-fibre foods
oatmeal	sugar-coated breakfast cereal
bran cereal	biscuit, scone, sweet roll
bran muffin	doughnut
wholemeal bread	white bread or cream crackers
brown rice	white rice
beans (fresh and dried)	mashed potatoes
bean soup	potato soup
fresh vegetables	chips

Lowering the blood fats
The HCF diet can lower your blood cholesterol by 20 to 30 per cent. It also lowers the blood triglycerides. These are the two major types of fat in our bodies – cholesterol and the triglycerides. Cholesterol is a special form of fat found in eggs, butter, cheese, meats, poultry, fish and dairy products. Triglycerides are storage fats found in animal products. They are stored in muscle and under the skin throughout the body. The fat under the skin of a hen or duck and the visible fat in bacon or on roast beef or steak, for example, is storage fat or triglycerides. These fats from foods, cholesterol and triglycerides, are carried in the bloodstream. The cholesterol is used by certain cells and excess is deposited in the arteries, so leading to hardening of the arteries and possibly heart attacks. The triglycerides are used for energy or fuel, and excessive amounts are stored in fatty tissue under the skin or in muscles.

How do you know if you have high blood fats?   Everyone needs to know what his or her blood cholesterol level is. If heart attacks at an early age (before the age of fifty) or blood cholesterol problems run in your family, you should make a special trip to the doctor to have your blood cholesterol measured. Otherwise, ask your doctor to measure your cholesterol the next time you have a blood test. Unfortunately many people do not learn that their blood cholesterol is too high until they have a heart attack; by then some damage is already done. It is better to find out as early as possible whether you have a cholesterol problem and then follow a diet and a suitable exercise routine to lower the cholesterol.

Everyone has some fat stores, but in excess they cause obesity. When people eat too many calories fat is stored in collections in muscle and under the skin. Men tend to develop a spare tyre or fatty accumulation around the waist, while women collect fat on the hips and thighs. A diet containing too much fat or triglycerides results in these fatty deposits.

How does the HCF diet help reduce blood fat levels? Soluble fibre reduces cholesterol in two ways. First, it increases the loss of bile acids. These acids are manufactured from cholesterol in the liver to aid in the digestion of fat. Soluble fibre increases the loss of the bile acids in the faeces, so acting to lower the blood cholesterol. The soluble fibre is also used by bacteria in the colon. These bacteria produce special acids from the fibre that travel to the liver and the acids turn off cholesterol production in the liver. Thus cholesterol loss as bile acids plus reduced manufacture of cholesterol combine to lower the blood cholesterol. Virtually all of the cholesterol in the blood is released from the liver; when the liver releases less cholesterol the blood cholesterol levels fall. The liver cannot compensate or readjust adequately – it undercompensates and the blood cholesterol remains lower.

Oat products and beans are specially effective in lowering the blood cholesterol because they are the richest food sources of soluble fibre. As we pointed out above, eating these foods as part of the HCF diet lowers it by as much as 30 per cent. Using this dietary approach, we have controlled the blood cholesterol of many people attending our clinic quite well. Often it means we can give less medication to regulate the blood cholesterol.

For people with high blood triglycerides, the HCF diet is very effective. It usually lowers them by 70 to 90 per cent and eliminates the need for medication – and the chances of undesirable side effects that go along with it. Control of the blood triglycerides with diet alone is much safer than with medication. We do not at present understand how the HCF diet lowers blood triglycerides, but part of the lowering effect is due to reduced fat intake. Another part may be related to the lower levels of insulin in the blood that the diet seems to promote (see page 12). Insulin, the hormone that helps the body burn sugar, also stimulates the manufacture of triglycerides. Thus to reduce blood triglycerides we use the HCF diet and recommend weight reduction, regular exercise and cutting out alcohol.

Hardening of the arteries

Heart attacks and strokes caused by the arteries getting clogged up (or hardening) are the major causes of death in our society. Exciting new research shows that lowering the blood fats leads to reversal of hardening of the arteries. X-ray pictures indicate that over a few months minor narrowing of the blood vessels (atherosclerosis) is improved by lowering the blood fats. As we have seen, the HCF diet does lower the blood fats, and so I feel that it is a wise diet for protecting against hardening of the arteries – and may sometimes even reverse the process.

Reducing high blood pressure

An improved diet and healthier lifestyle allow many people with high blood pressure to control their condition without medication. The main recommendation is to lower salt intake and there is certainly convincing evidence of the good effect of doing this (see *The Salt-Free Diet Book* by Dr Graham MacGregor, in this series). Eating a high-fibre diet is also beneficial. Evidence that people on a high-fibre intake, such as vegetarians, have lower blood pressure on average than people with low-fibre intake bears this out. We have also shown that increasing the fibre intake lowers blood pressure. With its emphasis on fruit and fresh vegetables, the HCF diet is automatically lower in salt and higher in potassium than the average Western diet. These changes in mineral intake certainly are not harmful, and may be beneficial. The diet actually lowered the blood pressure of people we treated by 10 per cent.

If there is high blood pressure in your family a restriction of salt intake combined with the HCF diet may protect you from this condition. If you have high blood pressure and are on medication for it, you may want to try the HCF diet plan as one way to control it without side effects. But you should not start a new diet or alter your medication without consulting your doctor first.

People with diabetes

The HCF diet lowers blood sugar and insulin needs in both insulin dependent and non-insulin dependent diabetics. In fact, as I have said, it was treating our diabetic patients that led to the development of the HCF diet. Studies in California, Oxford (England) and Denmark have confirmed our findings. The diet offers major advantages for non insulin-dependent diabetics since it almost always reduces the need for treatment by medication by making the body more sensitive to its own insulin, the hormone that promotes disposal of sugar in the body. The diet also lowers the blood fats that are a danger to the arteries, and helps in weight loss, so often necessary in adult diabetics. For the insulin-dependent diabetic, it smoothes out the blood sugar by slowing down its absorption. This results in a more comfortable and safer daily pattern. The diet may even lower insulin needs slightly (10 to 30 per cent).

Diabetes is much less common among peoples eating high-fibre diets than among people in Western countries who use fibre-depleted diets. If there is diabetes in your family, the HCF diet, staying slender and getting regular exercise may protect you from this condition. (*Diabetes, a Practical New Guide to Healthy Living* gives you detailed information about diabetes and the use of HCF diets specially for diabetics.)

Hundreds of people attending our clinic have enjoyed the HCF diet under my supervision and virtually all believe it is the best form of health insurance they can have. They feel better and have successfully lowered their blood fats and blood pressure. We carefully monitored the diet for ten years and are confident that it is a safe diet for lifelong use for anyone who is healthy and for people with the conditions I've described, provided they talk to their doctor about it. Regular exercise, proper relaxation and rest, and moderation in use of alcohol and coffee go with the HCF diet as a programme for health and well-being. Here are some hints on how to benefit best from it.

Getting the best from the HCF diet

1. You will need to shop more carefully and may need to prepare more vegetables than you do now. However, the HCF diet can save you money on food; people using it say their grocery bills are 20 per cent lower.

2. Exercise complements the HCF diet. It burns off calories faster, so promoting weight reduction, and it strengthens the heart. People who are unwell or out of condition must discuss with their doctor what exercise they may do. We recommend that fit people walk at least thirty minutes daily for six to eight weeks and then walk for thirty minutes three or four times weekly. Walking is one of your best exercises but jogging, if you are in good health, swimming or using an exercise bicycle also are good (for losing weight, see my recommendation on page 18).

3. Smoking is extremely harmful, especially to your heart and lungs. You should give it up altogether. Even the occasional cigarette has been shown to be bad, and the more you smoke, the greater the risks to your health.

4. Many people on the diet enjoy two glasses of wine or two cocktails containing about 25 ml/1 fl oz alcohol daily, with no adverse effects that we can measure. But excessive drinking is bad for you. It damages the liver and may damage the heart and cause high blood pressure, despite an otherwise healthy diet. Ten drinks per day provide 700 calories, which either displace other food or cause weight gain.

USING THE HCF DIET

Once you have decided the HCF diet will benefit you, and you have checked that it's all right with your doctor if you have a condition that needs monitoring, you can start your healthy eating programme right away. The ingredients and ways of preparing them for the HCF diet are so simple that even inexperienced cooks can easily produce a varied and tasty menu. The same applies if you're living alone and tend to fall back on convenience foods. You'll find the HCF diet easy and rewarding to prepare.

Plan your breakfast first. Start the day with fruit or juice, whole-grain cereal (made with oatflakes is my favourite), low-fat milk, wholemeal toast or a bran muffin. Centre your evening meal round wholemeal lasagne or spaghetti instead of roast beef. Start the meal with a soup, follow it with a green salad and have two of your favourite vegetables with the main dish. Select a hearty whole-grain bread to accompany your meal and finish with a fruit dessert and coffee.

If you don't eat at home at midday, lunch can be your biggest challenge. To begin with, you could have just a low-calorie salad, order a bowl of soup with crispbreads or have a vegetable platter. Later on you can take a wholemeal sandwich or a stew in a Thermos flask. Soon you'll be eating the HCF way and enjoying an enormous variety in your diet.

Shopping

1. Eat before shopping; this cuts down on impulse buying.

2. Use a shopping list. Plan your meals for the week and stick to your shopping list.

3. Select fresh fruit and vegetables and breads and cereals that have not been stripped of their natural fibrous coating. Buy wholemeal rather than white flour, brown rice rather than polished white rice, raw potatoes rather than instant mashed potatoes.

4. Try the store brands; often they provide equivalent quality at much lower prices than the highly advertised brands.

5. Examine the labels of products carefully. Try to select items that are low in sugar content and provide less than 30 per cent of calories from fat. Labels list the most common ingredients first and the least common last. For example, a tomato sauce label lists tomatoes, salt, dextrose and spices. Tomatoes are the main ingredient by weight and spices the least prevalent

item. This product is generous in salt, the second ingredient, has added sugar (dextrose) and has no added fat.

Don't forget that cereal products often list calories, protein, carbohydrate and fat per serving.

Oat products

Many of the recipes include oats and oat products because of their water-soluble fibre content. When following a recipe, be sure to use the correct type stated in that recipe. Raw oatmeal varies from pinhead, or coarse (ideal for traditional breakfast porridge), through medium to fine. These different types of oatmeal are right for making stuffings and baking. Rolled oats and jumbo oats are the faster-cooking flakes, usually steamed or precooked, often used in muesli and biscuits such as flapjacks. Toasted, they make a delicious topping (see page 89). Oat bran is the bran part of the oats alone – the highest in fibre. It usually includes the oat germ (eg, Mornflake Oatbran and Oatgerm), and it can be used to thicken stews or be sprinkled as it is on other foods to increase fibre content.

Milk and cheeses – which should you eat?

Skimmed milk provides the same protein, vitamins and minerals as does whole milk at half the calories. It has no fat or cholesterol and only 80 calories per 225 ml/8 fl oz. Low-fat milk has 1 to 2 per cent fat and 100 to 120 calories per 225 ml/8 fl oz, while whole milk has about 4 per cent fat and approximately 160 calories per 225 ml/8 fl oz. For adults I recommend the use of low-fat milk with 2 per cent or less fat to minimize animal fat and cholesterol intake. I use skimmed milk on my cereal and drink low-fat milk. When skimmed milk is unavailable you can make it from instant non-fat dried milk; mix this with whole milk or 2 per cent milk to make your own low-fat milk for drinking.

As a rule, eat low-fat or fat-free cheeses to avoid excessive animal fat and cholesterol. Cottage cheese is the lowest in fat, with about 1 per cent. Ricotta, curd cheese and fromage blanc or quark usually have a low-fat content too. These low-fat cheeses should have only 1 to 3 grams of fat per 25 g/1 oz and can be used for cooking. Part skimmed-milk cheeses such as mozzarella and some diet cheeses have approximately 5 grams of fat per 25 g/1 oz and should be used judiciously. To limit your cholesterol and fat intake, I recommend that you save your favourite high-fat cheeses (such as brie, cheddar, gouda, with over 5 g of fat per 25 g/1 oz) for occasional use only, say with fruit after a special meal.

Dressings

Avoid mayonnaise and bottled salad dressings such as French, Italian, Russian. They give you 110 to 140 calories per 25 g/1 oz with about 80 per cent of the calories from fat. Buy lower-calorie dressings or make your own using our recipes. Many grocery stores sell tasty salad dressings with only 20 to 40 calories per 25 g/

1 oz, or 10 to 20 calories per tablespoon serving. My favourite Italian herb dressing has only 8 calories per tablespoon. In the menu plan section I always recommend low-calorie dressings with less than 40 calories per 25 g/1 oz or 20 calories per tablespoon.

For mayonnaise and sour cream substitute plain low-fat yoghurt. The resulting dishes are much lower in fat and calories and taste better to me. My stomach complains when I eat too much fat.

Cooking suggestions

Meat, fish and poultry   Bake, grill, roast, stew or sauté when possible. These cooking methods require little added fat and remove some of the fat contained in red meats. Roasting or grilling beef or pork allows the fat to drip away. Try to avoid frying or deep frying since these processes tend to retain the fat or even add more, if the meat has a thick batter coating. Dry frying or sautéing can be done with very little fat – or none, if the meat has enough fat of its own. Trim all visible fat from meats and remove the skin from chicken before cooking.

Fats and oils   Use the minimum oil possible in cooking. For baking use vegetable oils, either corn or safflower for preference, instead of solid shortening, and try to reduce the amount. Many scones and breads can be made with less than half the fat content normally used. Replace butter on vegetables with a sprinkling of fresh herbs, for example parsley or chives.

Bouillon or stock   I personally have never seen anyone make beef stock. If you have the two to eleven hours required to watch the stock pot, you will have the best-flavoured dishes, I'm sure. For practical reasons the recipes list stock cubes or powder. Stock cubes are high in salt and even the instant or powdered bouillon has more salt than I recommend. Although this is not a low-salt cookery book, I have tried to keep the salt content of recipes to the lowest level practical. Watch for lower sodium – or salt – stock cubes, broths and soy sauces in health food shops. If you have been put on a low-sodium diet, follow instructions you have been given for making salt-free stock and omit soy sauce from the recipes.

Eggs   We don't use eggs at our house. One egg yolk has more cholesterol, 250 mg, than I usually eat in two or three days. Since a low dietary cholesterol intake lowers your blood cholesterol, I recommend that you avoid egg yolks. Substitute egg replacer (available from health food shops) or egg whites for whole eggs. The recipes show how both these may be used in cooking – but as egg replacer is not common in the UK we have also tested those needing it with egg white.

Sugar and sugar substitutes   Sugar, honey and fructose are refined sugars that are high in calories and low in vitamins, minerals and fibre. Sugars contribute to obesity, tooth decay and high blood fats. For these reasons the recipes use a minimum of sugar. We use saccharin and or the new substitute, aspartame, at our house to lower the calorie content of foods. But using sugar instead of sugar substitutes will not alter the outcome of most of the recipes in the book, if you wish to do so. As an alternative you can often use mashed fruit, dried fruit, concentrated fruit juice or dried unsweetened coconut instead of sugar.

Herbs and spices Herbs or spices enhance the flavour of vegetables, soups and salad dressings and decrease the need for salt and fat. I enjoy a large baked potato with freshly ground pepper and chopped chives. Sometimes I add a tablespoon of low-fat yoghurt.

Low-calorie fillers Vegetables and salads are the most important features of this diet. To lose weight and avoid getting hungry, use at least five servings of fresh or cooked vegetables daily (quantities are shown in the recipes and meal plans). Eat one or two large salads as well, with or without a low-calorie dressing. Use all forms of salad greens, cabbage or spinach, and other vegetables such as raw carrots and mushrooms to add variety and interest.

Vitamin B$_{12}$ The HCF diet includes a great variety of foods and meets all of your nutrient requirements. At calorie levels below 1500 per day this diet may be marginal in vitamin B$_{12}$ because of the limited use of liver and red meats. On a diet below 1500 calories, therefore, I recommend that you take one vitamin capsule daily to provide 5 micrograms of vitamin B$_{12}$.

LOSING WEIGHT THE HIGH-FIBRE WAY

If you want to lose weight, high-fibre foods are good choices for you. They are filling, decrease appetite between meals and cause some wastage of calories. Early in our research people coming to our clinic told us that the HCF diet was very filling; they could eat less food and still feel full. The diet helped many people shed 4.5 to 7 kg/10 to 15 lb of weight they did not need. In 1976 we began testing an 800-calorie diet that was high in fibre and carbohydrates and low in fat. We used it for middle-aged men being treated in our hospital who weighed about 112 kg/250 lb. These men lost 0.45 kg/1 lb a day (9.5 kg/21 lb in three weeks) but did not get hungry! Further studies showed that they were less hungry on 800-calorie high-fibre diets than on 800-calorie low-fibre diets. After leaving the hospital most men continued losing 0.5 to 1.3 kg/1 to 3 lb per week on the HCF diet.

If you are slightly overweight or somewhat obese (up to 22 kg/ 50 lb above the suggested weight), using the HCF diet plans outlined on pages 20–33, you should be able to lose weight gradually. Don't expect to lose a pound a day like the men in our research study; this diet was specially designed to produce rapid weight loss safely. But you can lose weight that will stay off if you are well-motivated, follow the diet and exercise regularly. (The table opposite gives recommended body weights for adults over 25 years old.)

If you are fairly obese or very obese do not start on the plan by yourself. You need careful medical supervision to lose weight properly.

The HCF weight-loss plan

Commitment   Promise yourself that you can control your appetite and follow a weight-loss programme. Buy a small notebook and write down *everything* you eat. This is the most effective way of regulating your calorie intake. Write down too how long you exercise each day. Avoid having snacks, tasting or nibbling. Since alcohol provides calories and stimulates the appetite, cut down or avoid it altogether.

Diet   Follow the HCF menu plan exactly. Eat three meals and a bedtime snack every day. Don't skip meals. For the first three weeks eat only the foods listed in the menu plan. Later on you can begin substituting similar foods to add variety to your diet. Avoid sweets, cakes and biscuits altogether. Limit the use of high-fat items such as nuts, cheeses, ice cream, pastries and high-calorie salad dressings.

Exercise   Most people cannot lose weight without burning up extra calories through exercise. Get extra exercise by walking briskly for at least thirty minutes twice a day. If you are not used to walking you may need to start gradually with ten minutes twice a day, building up to thirty minutes twice daily. Walking after meals uses even more calories than exercising on an empty stomach. During bad weather you might swim or use an exercise bicycle indoors.

How much weight will you lose?

A steady weight loss of 0.5 to 1 kg/1 to 2 lb a week is safe and likely

Recommended body weights
(*height without shoes; weight without clothes*)

Height		Men		Women	
cm	ft in	kg	lb	kg	lb
147	4 10			42–54	92–119
150	4 11			43–55	94–122
152	5 0			44–57	96–125
155	5 1			45–58	99–128
157	5 2	51–64	112–141	46–59	102–131
160	5 3	52–65	115–144	48–61	105–134
163	5 4	54–67	118–148	49–63	108–138
165	5 5	55–69	121–152	50–64	111–142
168	5 6	56–71	124–156	52–66	114–146
170	5 7	58–73	128–161	53–68	118–150
173	5 8	60–75	132–166	55–70	122–154
175	5 9	62–77	136–170	57–72	126–158
178	5 10	63–79	140–174	59–74	130–163
180	5 11	65–81	144–179	61–76	134–168
183	6 0	67–83	148–184	63–78	138–173
185	6 1	69–86	152–189		
188	6 2	71–87	156–194		
190	6 3	73–89	160–199		
193	6 4	74–92	164–204		

Source: U.S. Department of Health, Education and Welfare Conference on Obesity, 1973

to be maintained. Avoid crash diets containing fewer than 800 calories per day.

Your calorie needs are based on your weight, activity level and rate of metabolism. The table overleaf gives you an idea of rates of weight loss on the different diets. In each instance I assume that you follow the diet very closely and walk for thirty minutes twice a day.

Everyone is different. I cannot guarantee you will lose weight with the HCF plan – although with the exception of short, middle-aged women, everyone attending my clinic can lose weight on 1000 calories. Remember, exercise is just as important as diet. If you want to lose weight more rapidly, exercise more than outlined above. Don't cheat on the diet until you have lost at least 4.5 kg/10 lb and are confident you can continue to lose weight nicely. When you reach your goal weight, increase your calories to the next level (for example, go from 1000 to 1500 calories) to main-

Present weight	HCF diet	Minimum expected weight loss
kg/lb	KCals/calories	kg/lb per week
54/120	1000	0.5/1
63/140	1000	0.7/1½
72/160	1000	1/2
81/180	1500	0.7/1½
90/200	1500	1/2
over 90/200	2000	0.5–1/1–2

tain that weight. The HCF diet is designed for long-term health maintenance, but it can't continue to benefit you if you go back to eating too many of the high-energy and fat foods – though I doubt you'll want to!

On the next pages we give recommended menu plans for each of the diets, using recipes in this book.

MEAL PLANS

Dishes marked with an asterisk appear in the recipes, pages 34–118.

Weights and measures
The recipe ingredients are in both metric and Imperial measurements. Slight roundings up have been made, so do not mix the two in any one recipe.

The spoon measurements are level unless otherwise stated. One teaspoon (tsp) = 5 ml; 1 tablespoon (tbsp) = 15 ml. To ensure success, check the size of the spoons you are using.

Australian users should remember that as their tablespoon has been converted to 20 ml, and is therefore larger than the tablespoon measurement used in the recipes in this book, they should use 3 × 5 ml tsp where instructed to use 1 × 15 ml tbsp.

The energy value per serving is given in kilocalories (Kcal). Kilocalories are commonly known as calories.

The 1000-calorie diet
The 1000-calorie HCF plan will maintain the body weight of middle-aged or elderly women of about 45 kg/100 lb. It will be a weight-reducing diet for anyone weighing over 54 kg/120 lb. With

this plan you should include one vitamin tablet daily providing vitamin B_6 and vitamin B_{12} supplements.

The basic menu plan for the 1000-calorie diet includes the following: one serving of hot or cold cereal, 335 ml/12 fl oz of skimmed milk, 3 servings of low-calorie vegetables (50 g/2 oz of, for example, cooked carrots, green beans), 2 servings of other garden vegetables (140 g/5 oz tomatoes or beetroot), 2 servings of starchy vegetables (50 g/2 oz sweetcorn, peas, potatoes or rice), 1 serving of dried beans (115 g/4 oz cooked or tinned haricot or red kidney beans), 3 slices of bread, 15 ml/1 tbsp of margarine, 75 g/3 oz of beef or pork *or* 170 g/6 oz of fish, and 3 servings of fruit. This provides you with a great deal of food and with a wide variety of choices. I have given you examples of daily menus but you can work out your own plan to meet your own food preferences. Remember, however, you must eat three main meals and an evening snack each day to get the full benefit of this plan.

Basic meal plan for the 1000-calorie diet

Breakfast Fresh fruit, 1 serving *or* fruit juice, 115 ml/4 fl oz
           Hot or cold cereal, 1 serving
           Skimmed milk, 225 ml/8 fl oz
           Wholemeal toast, 1 slice
           Margarine, 5 ml/1 tsp

Lunch   Vegetable juice, 115 ml/4 fl oz
           Bean soup *or* Chilli,* 1 serving
           Boiled cabbage, 50 g/2 oz
           Wholemeal crispbread, 3
           Fresh fruit, 1 serving

Dinner   Large green salad with low-calorie salad dressing
           Baked fish, 150 g/5 oz
           Brown rice, 75 g/3 oz
           Carrots, 50 g/2 oz
           Asparagus, 115 g/4 oz
           Fruit dessert, 1 serving, with yoghurt topping,
             25 g/1 oz

Snack   Popcorn, 115 g/4 oz, popped *or* fresh vegetable platter
             with celery, carrot and courgette sticks, and Curry
             vegetable dip* with rye crispbread, 2

Menu 1

Breakfast Grapefruit, ½
           Porridge, 1 serving
           Skimmed milk, 225 ml/8 fl oz

Lunch   Main meal salad with low-calorie salad dressing
           Turkey-rice sauté,* 1 serving
           Broccoli, cooked, 50 g/2 oz
           Peach, 1 medium

Dinner   Chilled mixed vegetable juice, 115 ml/4 fl oz
Summer-light tuna salad,* 1 serving, served on lettuce
Green beans, 75 g/3 oz
Oat bran muffin,* 1
Seedless grapes, 10

Snack   Wholemeal crispbread, 3, with low-sugar strawberry
preserve, 10 ml/2 tsp

Menu 2

Breakfast Melon, ½
Shredded Wheat, 50 g/2 oz
Skimmed milk, 225 ml/ 8 fl oz

Lunch   Gazpacho,* 1 serving
Summer-light tuna salad,* 1 serving
Wholemeal crispbread, 3
Pear, 1 small

Dinner   Main meal salad with tomatoes and low-calorie salad
dressing
Broccoli-ham rollups,* 1 serving
Corn on the cob, 1 medium ear
Cooked carrots, 50 g/2 oz
Wholemeal bread, 1 slice
Frozen fruit salad,* 1 serving

Snack   Celery, carrot, courgette sticks with Curry vegetable
dip,* 1 serving

Menu 3

Breakfast Apple sauce porridge,* 1 serving with raisins,
10 ml/2 tsp
Skimmed milk, 225 ml/8 fl oz

Lunch   Tomato juice, 115 ml/4 fl oz
Tostadas,* 1
Brown rice, 75 g/3 oz
Apple, 1

Dinner   Spinach salad,* 1 serving
Lemon baked fish,* 1 serving
Marrow, 50 g/2 oz
Cooked beetroot, 50 g/2 oz
Wholemeal bread, 1 slice
Peach crumble,* 1 serving, with yoghurt topping,
50 g/2 oz

Snack   Fresh vegetable platter with celery, cucumber and
radishes and seasoning salt

Menu 4

Breakfast   Orange, 1 small
100 per cent or All-Bran cereal, 25 g/1 oz
Skimmed milk, 225 ml/8 fl oz

Lunch   Green salad with low-calorie salad dressing
Turkey sandwich: sliced turkey, 25 g/1 oz, sliced
   tomato, lettuce, alfalfa sprouts, wholemeal bread, 2
   slices, low-calorie salad dressing, 5 ml/1 tsp
Peach, 1 medium

Dinner   Cooked spinach, 75 g/3 oz
Macaroni casserole,* 1 serving
Creamed beetroot,* 1 serving
Wholemeal bread, 1 slice
Fresh fruit salad,* 1 serving

Snack   Digestive biscuits, 2

Menu 5

Breakfast   Grapefruit, ½
Porridge, 1 serving
Skimmed milk, 225 ml/8 fl oz

Lunch   Bean soup,* 1 serving
Vegetarian sandwich*: sandwich filling and rye bread,
   1 slice
Fresh strawberries, 170 g/6 oz

Dinner   Main meal salad, tomatoes and low-calorie salad
   dressing
Beef kebab,* 1 serving
Baked potato, 1 medium with low-fat plain
   yoghurt, 50 ml/2 fl oz, and chopped chives
Green beans with water chestnuts,* 1 serving
Spiced peaches,* 1 serving

Snack   Fresh vegetable platter with cauliflower florets,
   mushrooms and courgettes with Curry vegetable dip,*
   1 serving

Menu 6

Breakfast   Strawberries, 170 g/6 oz with Grapenuts, 45 ml/3 tbsp,
   low-fat plain yoghurt, 115 ml/4 fl oz, and artificial
   sweetener to taste

Lunch   Vegetable juice, 115 ml/4 fl oz
Cheese sandwich: low-fat cheese, 25 g/1 oz, sliced
   tomato, lettuce, alfalfa sprouts, low-calorie salad
   dressing, 5 ml/1 tsp, wholemeal bread, 2 slices

Dinner	Main meal salad with low-calorie salad dressing
	Parmigiana,* 1 serving
	Wholemeal spaghetti, 115 g/4 oz, with parmesan cheese, 15 ml/1 tbsp, and margarine, 5 ml/1 tsp
	Broccoli, cooked, 50 g/2 oz
	Pear with melba sauce,* 1 serving
Snack	Strawberries, 75 g/3 oz, with yoghurt, 50 g/2 oz

Menu 7

Breakfast	Orange juice, 115 ml/ 4 fl oz
	Porridge, 1 serving, with 10 ml/2 tsp low-sugar strawberry preserve
	Skimmed milk, 225 ml/8 fl oz
Lunch	Green salad with low-calorie salad dressing
	Baked beef and potato,* 1 serving
	Green beans, 50 g/2 oz
	Pear, 1
Dinner	Oriental garden salad,* 1 serving
	Cantonese prawns,* 1 serving
	Wholemeal bread, 1 slice
	Margarine, 5 ml/1 tsp
	Satsuma, 75 g/3 oz
Snack	Popcorn, 115 g/4 oz, popped, sprinkled lightly with parmesan cheese

The 1500-calorie diet

The basic meal plan for 1500 calories includes: 1 serving of hot or cold cereal, 450 ml/16 fl oz of low-fat milk, 7 servings of vegetables, 2 servings of starchy vegetables (50 g/2 oz sweetcorn, peas, potatoes or rice), 1–2 servings of dried beans (115 g/4 oz cooked or tinned haricot or red kidney beans), 7 slices of bread, 25 ml/5 tsp of margarine or salad dressing, 75–115 g/3–4 oz of beef, pork, chicken or fish, and 3–4 servings of fruit each day. This plan will maintain a stable body weight for many young women weighing about 53 kg/115 lb, for middle-aged women weighing 54–63 kg/120–140 lb and for middle-aged men weighing about 59 kg/130 lb. If you are heavier than this you should lose weight on 1500 calories.

Basic meal plan for the 1500-calorie diet

Breakfast Cereal, hot or cold
Skimmed milk, 225 ml/8 fl oz
Fruit *or* fruit juice
Muffin
Margarine

Lunch Tomato *or* vegetable juice
Salad with low-calorie salad dressing
Sandwich: wholemeal bread, turkey *or* vegetarian
   filling, low-calorie salad dressing
Garden vegetable
Fruit

Dinner Vegetable soup
Salad with low-calorie salad dressing
Main course casserole: meat, fish *or* poultry
Potatoes, rice *or* corn
Bean dish
Garden vegetable
Wholemeal bread or muffin
Margarine
Fruit dessert

Snack Digestive biscuit *or* muffin
Raw vegetables

Menu 1

Breakfast Grapefruit, ½
Three-grain waffles,* 1 serving
Hot orange sauce,* 1 serving
Skimmed milk, 115 ml/4 fl oz

Lunch Lettuce, ¼ head with low-calorie salad dressing
Oriental chicken,* 1 serving
Brown rice, 75 g/3 oz
Broccoli, 75 g/3 oz
Sour-dough oat bread,* 1 serving
Margarine, 5 ml/1 tsp
Gingered fruit salad,* 1 serving

Dinner Tomato juice cocktail, 115 ml/4 fl oz
Cheesy garden casserole,* 1 serving
Green beans, 50 g/2 oz
Wholemeal bread, 1 slice
Margarine, 5 ml/1 tsp
Strawberries, 75 g/3 oz with low-fat plain yoghurt, 30
   ml/2 tbsp sweetened to taste with artificial sweetener

Snack   Grapenut cereal, 45 ml/3 tbsp with strawberries,
              75 g/3 oz and skimmed milk, 115 ml/4 fl oz

Menu 2

Breakfast   Orange juice, 115 ml/4 fl oz
            Porridge, 1 serving
            Skimmed milk, 115 ml/4 fl oz
            Blackberry muffin,* 1

Lunch   Fresh vegetable platter with carrots, celery, radishes
            and seasoned salt
            Bavarian beans,* 1 serving
            Cornmeal muffin,* 1
            Margarine, 5 ml/1 tsp
            Apple, 1 small

Dinner   Green salad with tomatoes and low-calorie salad
            dressing
            Sole Florentine,* 1 serving
            Baked marrow, ½ with margarine, 5 ml/1 tsp, and sugar
            substitute
            Green beans, 115 g/4 oz
            Cornmeal muffin,* 1
            Margarine, 5 ml/1 tsp
            Hot fruit compote,* 1 serving

Snack   Creamy rice pudding,* 1 serving
            Digestive biscuits, 2

Menu 3

Breakfast   Melon, ½
            Bran flakes, 50 g/2 oz
            Skimmed milk, 225 ml/8 fl oz
            Oat muffin,* 1
            Margarine, 10 ml/2 tsp

Lunch   Tomato juice, 115 ml/4 fl oz
            Pitta bread sandwich,* 1 serving
            Rice-fruit salad,* 1 serving

Dinner   Gazpacho,* 1 serving
            Chicken and rice,* 1 serving
            Green beans, 115 g/4 oz
            Sweetcorn casserole,* 1 serving
            Wholemeal bread, 2 slices
            Margarine, 5 ml/1 tsp
            Peach, 1 medium

Snack   Split pea soup,* 1 serving
            Wholemeal crispbread, 3

Menu 4

Breakfast Grapefruit, ½
Porridge, 1 serving
Skimmed milk, 75 ml/3 fl oz
Banana bread,* 1 slice
Margarine, 5 ml/1 tsp

Lunch Carrot, celery and courgette sticks with Curry
vegetable dip,* 1 serving
Chilli,* 1 serving
Pear, 1 small

Dinner Green salad with low-calorie salad dressing
Beef kebab,* 1 serving
Green beans, 115 g/4 oz
Lemon carrots,* 1 serving
Baked potato, 1 medium with chives and low-fat plain
yoghurt, 30 ml/2 tbsp
Buttermilk rolls,* 3
Fresh fruit salad,* 1 serving

Snack Jim's instant breakfast,* 1 serving

Menu 5

Breakfast Orange juice, 115 ml/4 fl oz
Porridge, 1 serving
Skimmed milk, 225 ml/8 fl oz
Bran muffin,* 1
Margarine, 5 ml/1 tsp

Lunch Vegetable juice, 115 ml/4 fl oz
Italian bean salad,* 1 serving
Rye bread, 2 slices
Margarine, 5 ml/1 tsp

Dinner Summer salad,* 1 serving
Honey-curried fish,* 1 serving
Baked mushroom rice,* 1 serving
Green beans, 50 g/2 oz
Sour-dough oat bread,* 1 slice
Margarine, 5 ml/1 tsp
Apple crumble,* 1 serving

Snack Popcorn, 115 g/4 oz, popped, with margarine,
10 ml/2 tsp

Menu 6

Breakfast Apple juice, 115 ml/4 fl oz
Cornflakes, 25 g/1 oz
Skimmed milk, 225 ml/8 fl oz
Bran muffin,* 1
Margarine, 5 ml/1 tsp

Lunch Green salad with low-calorie salad dressing
Chilli con carne,* 1 serving
Quickly pickled beetroot,* 1 serving
Wholemeal crispbread, 3
Seedless grapes, 10

Dinner Fresh fruit salad,* 1 serving
Meat loaf,* 1 serving
Coleslaw,* 1 serving
Green beans, 115 g/4 oz
Baked apple,* 1 serving

Snack Quickly pickled beetroot,* 1 serving
Rye crispbread, 2

Menu 7

Breakfast Strawberries, 75 g/3 oz, with low-fat plain yoghurt,
30 ml/2 tbsp, sweetened to taste with artificial
sweetener
Spanish omelette,* 1 serving, *or* Orange French toast,
2 slices
Wholemeal toast, 1 slice
Margarine, 5 ml/1 tsp

Lunch Bean salad,* 1 serving
Tacos,* 1 serving
Spanish rice,* 1 serving
Peaches, tinned in own juice, 50 g/2 oz

Dinner Green salad with low-calorie salad dressing
Ratatouille,* 1 serving
Cumin rice,* 1 serving
Wholemeal bread, 1 slice
Margarine, 5 ml/1 tsp
Peachy fruit dessert,* 1 serving

Snack Grapenut cereal, 30 g/2 tbsp, over strawberries,
75 g/3 oz, topped with skimmed milk, 115 ml/4 fl oz,
sweetened to taste with artificial sweetener

The 2000-calorie diet

The basic meal plan for 2000 calories includes: 1–2 servings of hot or cold cereal, 450 ml/16 fl oz of low-fat milk, 6–7 servings of vegetables, 3 servings of starchy vegetables (50 g/2 oz sweetcorn, peas, potatoes or rice), 1–2 servings of dried beans (115 g/4 oz cooked or tinned haricot, Mexican or red kidney beans), 8 slices of bread, 35 ml/7 tsp of margarine or salad dressing, 115–170 g/4–6 oz of beef, pork, chicken or fish, and 4–6 servings of fruit a day. This plan will maintain a stable body weight for many young men weighing 63–68 kg/140–150 lb and for middle-aged men weighing 72–77 kg/160–170 lb. If you weigh more than this you should lose weight on 2000 calories.

If you are very active and lean you can maintain your present weight by following the menu plan and having larger servings of the suggested foods.

Basic meal plan for the 2000-calorie diet

Breakfast   Cereal, hot or cold
Skimmed milk, 225 ml/8 fl oz
Fruit *or* fruit juice
Breakfast bread *or* muffins
Margarine

Lunch   Salad with low-calorie salad dressing
Bean, barley *or* vegetable soup
Sandwich: wholemeal bread with low-calorie salad
dressing, cheese, turkey *or* lean meat *or* pizza *or*
pasta dish
Garden vegetables
Margarine
Fruit

Dinner   Tomato *or* vegetable juice
Soup *or* main meal salad with low-calorie salad
dressing
Main course casserole: meat, fish *or* poultry
Mixed vegetable casserole: corn, peas *or* potatoes
Bean dish
Wholemeal bread *or* muffins
Margarine
Dessert

Snack   Dry cereal with fruit and low-fat plain yoghurt
Muffin

Menu 1

Breakfast   Grapefruit, ½
            Spanish omelette,* 1 serving, *or* Orange French toast,
               2 slices
            Wholemeal toast, 2 slices
            Margarine, 5 ml/1 tsp
            Skimmed milk, 225 ml/8 fl oz
Lunch   Fruit cup,* 1 serving
            Pollo cacciatore,* 1 serving
            Spinach stir-fry,* 1 serving
            Hearty bean bake,* 1 serving
            Sour-dough oat bread,* 2 slices
            Margarine, 5 ml/1 tsp
            Apple crumble,* 1 serving, with low-fat plain yoghurt
               topping, 30 ml/2 tbsp, sweetened to taste with
               artificial sweetener
Dinner   Green salad with low-calorie salad dressing
            Beef and rice dinner,* 1 serving
            Asparagus delight,* 1 serving
            Carrot purée,* 1 serving
            Wholemeal muffin,* 1
            Margarine, 5 ml/1 tsp
            Strawberries, 75 g/3 oz, with low-fat plain yoghurt,
               30 ml/2 tbsp, sweetened to taste with artificial
               sweetener
Snack   Grapenut cereal, 45 g/3 tbsp, over strawberries,
               75 g/3 oz, topped with skimmed milk, 115 ml/4 fl oz,
               sweetened to taste with artificial sweetener

Menu 2

Breakfast   Orange juice, 115 ml/4 fl oz
            Porridge, 1 serving
            Skimmed milk, 225 ml/8 fl oz
            Blackberry muffin,* 1
            Margarine, 5 ml/1 tsp
Lunch   Split pea soup,* 1 serving
            Broccoli-ham rollups,* 1 serving
            German hot potato salad,* 1 serving
            Stewed tomatoes, 140 g/5 oz
            Wholemeal bread, 1 slice
            Orange and apple sauce salad*
Dinner   Spinach salad,* 1 serving
            Lemon baked fish,* 1 serving
            Stuffed tomatoes,* 1 serving
            Quickly pickled beetroot,* 1 serving
            Baked potato, 1 medium with plain low-fat yoghurt,
               30 ml/2 tbsp, and chopped chives

Sour-dough oat bread,* 1 slice
Margarine, 5 ml/1 tsp
Peach crumble,* 1 serving

Snack   Sour-dough oat bread,* 1 slice with low-sugar strawberry preserve, 15 ml/1 tbsp
Skimmed milk, 115 ml/4 fl oz

Menu 3

Breakfast Melon, ½
Oatmeal pancakes,* 3 medium
Fruit syrup, 45 ml/3 tbsp
Skimmed milk, 225 ml/8 fl oz
Margarine, 5 ml/1 tsp

Lunch   Green salad with low-calorie salad dressing
Chilli,* 1 serving
Fresh vegetable platter: celery, radishes, courgette
with Vegetable spread,* 1 serving
Cornmeal muffin,* 1
Orange, 1 medium

Dinner   Tomato juice cocktail,* 1 serving
Surprise meat balls,* 1 serving
Baked marrow,* 1 serving
Asparagus, 50 g/2 oz
Wholemeal bread, 2 slices
Margarine, 5 ml/1 tsp
Pears, tinned, 115 g/4 oz
Oat spice biscuits,* 2

Snack   Granola,* 1 serving
Skimmed milk, 225 ml/8 fl oz

Menu 4

Breakfast Grapefruit juice, 115 ml/4 fl oz
Orange French toast,* 3 slices
Low-sugar strawberry preserve, 45 ml/3 tbsp
Margarine, 15 ml/1 tbsp
Skimmed milk, 225 ml/8 fl oz

Lunch   Bean soup,* 2 servings
Stuffed tomatoes,* 1 serving
Wholemeal crispbread, 3
Strawberries, 75 g/3 oz, with low-fat plain yoghurt,
30 ml/2 tbsp, sweetened to taste with artificial
sweetener

Dinner   Green salad with tomatoes and low-calorie salad
dressing
Chicken with peaches,* 1 serving

Vegetable medley,* 1 serving
Wholemeal muffin,* 1
Margarine, 10 ml/2 tsp
Apple crumble,* 1 serving

Snack   Orange muesli,* 1 serving

Menu 5

Breakfast Orange juice, 115 ml/4 fl oz
Porridge, 1 serving
Skimmed milk, 115 ml/4 fl oz
Banana bread,* 1 serving
Margarine, 5 ml/1 tsp

Lunch   Fruited rice,* 1 serving on lettuce leaves
Asparagus, 115 g/4 oz
Wholemeal bread, 1 slice
Margarine, 5 ml/1 tsp
Oatmeal biscuits,* 2
Skimmed milk, 225 ml/8 fl oz

Dinner   Oriental garden salad,* 1 serving
Oriental kebabs,* 1 serving
Baked potato, 1 medium with low-fat plain yoghurt,
    30 ml/2 tbsp, with chopped chives
Beetroot, 50 g/2 oz
Courgette special,* 1 serving
Wholemeal bread, 1 slice
Margarine, 5 ml/1 tsp
Tropical fruit salad,* 1 serving

Snack   Chilli,* 1 serving
Wholemeal crispbread, 3

Menu 6

Breakfast Grapefruit, ½
Orange muesli,* 1 serving
Skimmed milk, 225 ml/8 fl oz
Blackberry muffin,* 1
Margarine, 5 ml/1 tsp

Lunch   Split pea soup,* 1 serving
Pitta bread sandwich:* turkey, 25 g/1 oz, and low-
    calorie salad dressing, 30 ml/2 tbsp
Apple, 1

Dinner   Tomato juice cocktail,* 115 ml/4 fl oz
Creamed chicken,* 1 serving
Golden pilaff,* 1 serving
Asparagus, 50 g/2 oz
Quickly pickled beetroot,* 1 serving
Wholemeal bread, 2 slices

Margarine, 5 ml/1 tsp
Crunchy bananas,* 1 serving

Snack   Grapenut cereal, 45 ml/3 tbsp, with strawberries,
170 g/6 oz, and low-fat plain yoghurt, 140 ml/5 fl oz,
sweetened to taste with artificial sweetener

Menu 7

Breakfast Melon, ½
Three-grain waffles,* 2 servings
Hot orange sauce,* 60 ml/4 tbsp
Margarine, 10 ml/2 tsp

Lunch   Gazpacho,* 1 serving
Tijuana pie,* 1 serving
Mexican fruit salad,* 1 serving
Wholemeal crispbread, 6
Pear, 1

Dinner   Green salad with tomatoes and low-calorie salad
dressing
Sole Florentine,* 1 serving
Marrow, baked, with margarine 10 ml/2 tsp, and
brown sugar 15 ml/1 tbsp
Green beans, 170 g/6 oz
Sour-dough oat bread,* 1 slice
Margarine, 10 ml/2 tsp
Strawberries, 170 g/6 oz, with low-fat plain yoghurt,
140 ml/5 fl oz, sweetened to taste with artificial
sweetener

Snack   Bean soup,* 1 serving
Rye crispbread, 2

BREAKFAST

Breakfast is the most important meal of the day. The old saying,
'Eat breakfast like a king, lunch like a prince and dinner like a
pauper', provides good advice for healthy eating. There is no substitute for a good breakfast. Before it your blood sugar is rather
low and your body machinery is operating at an idle speed. A good
breakfast raises your blood sugar and helps you get your body
machinery into high gear. A healthy helping of fruit, porridge or a
whole-grain cereal, low-fat milk, a bran muffin and tea or coffee
will sustain a good energy level until the midday meal.

For breakfast I usually have orange juice, porridge, skimmed milk and tea. When I have a very active day planned I will also have a bran muffin. I flavour my porridge with raisins, crunchy Grapenut cereal, low-sugar strawberry jam or artificial sweetener.

Although I have the same thing for breakfast almost every day, I know some people like more variety, so I have included suggestions for a number of different breakfasts. You can add a tasty blended fruit drink, a breakfast bread such as banana bread, or fruit and yoghurt. You can make your own low-calorie muesli with rolled oats; these have already been precooked so you are not getting 'raw' oats.

Cooking porridge

As we explained in the introduction, there are several different types of oatmeal available, and the method of making porridge varies according to the oatmeal you are using. Directions are usually given on the packet, but here are some general guidelines.

Coarse and medium oatmeal   For 4 people, allow 50 g/2 oz oatmeal. Bring 575 ml/1 pint lightly salted water to the boil. Stir in the oatmeal and continue stirring until it shows signs of thickening. Cover tightly, reduce the heat and simmer to required thickness (about 15–20 minutes).

Rolled (quick-cooking oats)   Take 25 g/1 oz per serving. Measure in a cup, then take twice the quantity of water and a pinch of salt. Combine and bring to the boil, stirring for 1 minute only.

Oatmeal and whole-grain cereals can also be cooked overnight in a slow cooker or, using a double boiler, you can cook your porridge while getting dressed and not have to stir it. Old-fashioned oatmeal or other types that require longer to cook have much more flavour; take the time and you can make porridge-lovers of the entire family. Taking time for breakfast gives you and your family a head start on the day.

Oatmeal pancakes

Makes 10 medium pancakes
Per serving: 71 KCal, 9 g carbohydrate, 3.6 g protein, 2.3 g fat, 1 mg cholesterol, 1.8 g fibre, 186 mg sodium

130 g/4½ oz rolled oats
15 ml/1 tbsp wholemeal flour
15 ml/1 tbsp baking powder

335 ml/12 fl oz skimmed milk
2 egg whites
15 ml/1 tbsp vegetable oil

Mix all the ingredients together. Lightly whisk the liquid ingredients and add to the dry. Stir until just combined. Let the mixture stand for 5 minutes. Lightly oil and heat a non-stick frying pan, and cook the pancakes turning when edges are firm. Grease the pan between each pancake if necessary.

Orange muesli

Serves 6
Per serving: 188 KCal, 27.2 g carbohydrate, 5.1 g protein, 6.5 g fat, 0 mg cholesterol, 5.9 g fibre, 4 mg sodium

170 g/6 oz jumbo oats
2 medium oranges, peeled and chopped
170 ml/6 fl oz orange juice
25 g/1 oz chopped nuts
40 g/1½ oz raisins
25 g/1 oz shredded coconut

Combine all the ingredients in a medium bowl with 225 ml/8 fl oz water; mix well. Cover and refrigerate overnight or for at least 8 hours. Mix well before serving.

Granola cereal

Serves 12
Per serving: 137 KCal, 19.4 g carbohydrate, 3.8 g protein, 4.9 g fat, 0 mg cholesterol, 4 g fibre, 3 mg sodium

335 g/12 oz jumbo oats
50 g/2 oz wholemeal flour
25 g/1 oz coconut, shredded
50 g/2 oz nuts, chopped
335 ml/12 fl oz apple juice
75 g/3 oz raisins

Heat oven to 180°C/350°F/gas 4.
Mix the oats, flour, half the coconut and the nuts in a large bowl. Pour in the apple juice and mix well. Spread out on baking sheets and bake for 30–40 minutes or until golden brown and crunchy; stir occasionally.
Stir in the raisins and remaining coconut during cooling. Keep refrigerated.

Apple sauce porridge

Serves 2
Per serving: 146 KCal, 25.2 g carbohydrate, 7.1 g protein, 1.9 g fat, 2 mg cholesterol, 4.1 g fibre, 64 mg sodium

225 ml/8 fl oz skimmed milk
40 g/1½ oz rolled oats
115 g/4 oz apple sauce, unsweetened
2.5 ml/½ tsp artificial sweetener
1.25 ml/¼ tsp powdered cinnamon
3 drops vanilla essence

Heat the milk over a medium heat until just ready to boil. Add the oats and stir until thickened. Add the apple sauce, sweetener, cinnamon and vanilla. Can be served without milk.

Orange French toast

Serves 4
Per serving: 118 KCal, 13.7 g carbohydrate, 5.9 g protein, 4.4 g fat, 0 mg cholesterol, 1.3 fibre, 187 mg sodium

egg replacer, equivalent to 2 eggs or 2　*2.5 ml/½ tsp vanilla essence*
　egg whites　*4 slices wholemeal bread*
85 ml/3 fl oz orange juice

Beat the egg replacer or whites, orange juice and vanilla essence together. Dip bread in batter to coat both sides. Lightly grease a non-stick frying pan and cook the slices until brown.
　Serve with a little margarine, puréed strawberries, low-calorie strawberry jam or hot orange sauce (see page 115).

Three-grain waffle

Makes 8
Per serving: 195 KCal, 28.3 g carbohydrate, 6.7 g protein, 6.1 g fat, 0 mg cholesterol, 6.9 g fibre, 39 mg sodium

50 g/2 oz cashew or other nuts　*75 g/3 oz wholemeal flour*
225 g/8 oz rolled oats　*140 g/5 oz cornmeal*

Finely chop nuts in a liquidizer or blender goblet. Add the oats and blend until a coarse flour is produced. Add the other ingredients to the blender and mix well. Transfer to a bowl. Add 875 ml/1½ pints hot water and stir until thoroughly combined. Bake on a hot lightly greased waffle iron for at least 8 minutes.

Tropical smoothie

Serves 2
Per serving: 135 KCal, 27.8 g carbohydrate, 3.8 g protein, 1 g fat, 0 mg cholesterol, 4.4 g fibre, 2 mg sodium

225 ml/8 fl oz orange juice　*40 g/1½ oz rolled oats*
1 ripe medium banana　*4 ice cubes*

Place all ingredients in a liquidizer or blender goblet. Blend on high speed for about 1 minute or until ice melts.

Banana cashew shake (*top*, see page 38), Tropical smoothie (*centre right*), Orange French toast with hot orange sauce (*centre left*, see above and page 115), Three-grain waffle with puréed strawberries (*bottom*)

Banana cashew shake   See photograph, page 37

Serves 2
Per serving: 261 KCal, 25.6 g carbohydrate, 9.6 g protein, 13.4 g
fat, 2 mg cholesterol, 2.4 g fibre, 67 mg sodium

225 ml/8 fl oz skimmed milk   *5 ml/1 tsp vanilla essence (optional)*
1 banana   *50 g/2 oz cashews*

Liquidize or blend together the skimmed milk, banana and vanilla
essence. Add the cashews, and blend again at high speed, until
smooth.

Spanish omelette

Serves 2
Per serving: 277 KCal, 24.7 g carbohydrate, 14 g protein, 13.6 g fat,
0 mg cholesterol, 0.3 g fibre, 231 mg sodium

5 ml/1 tsp margarine   *2.5 ml/½ tsp Worcestershire sauce*
30 ml/2 tbsp spring onion, chopped   *egg replacer, equivalent to 3 eggs*
30 ml/2 tbsp green pepper, chopped   *pinch of pepper*
30 ml/2 tbsp tomato purée, mixed
  with its own volume of water

Melt margarine in a frying pan. Add the spring onion and green
pepper. Cook until tender. Add the tomato purée and Worcestershire sauce. Simmer 5 to 7 minutes. Keep warm on low heat. Beat
the egg replacer with 30 ml/2 tbsp water and the pepper. Pour the
egg mixture into a non-stick omelette pan. Cook on medium heat
without stirring. When the omelette is brown on the bottom and
almost firm on top, spoon half the sauce over half the omelette.
Fold the other side of the omelette over. Cut in half and place on
two serving plates. Spoon the remaining sauce over each portion
and serve immediately.

Jim's instant breakfast

Serves 1
Per serving: 182 KCal, 32.7 g carbohydrate, 8.7 g protein, 1.8 g fat,
2 mg cholesterol, 5.2 g fibre, 151 mg sodium

25 g/1 oz jumbo oats   *1.25 ml/¼ tsp artificial sweetener*
30 ml/2 tbsp Grapenut cereal   *(optional)*
12 g/½ oz raisins   *115 ml/4 fl oz skimmed milk*

Mix the dry ingredients in bowl and add the milk. Allow to soak
for about 5 minutes.

Alternatives Use 25 g/1 oz raisin bran cereal instead of Grapenuts.

Substitute half a banana, sliced, or 50 g/2 oz strawberries for the raisins.

BREADS AND BISCUITS

Bread is aptly called the 'staff of life'. Bread is one of your best food choices. Whole-grain breads are excellent sources of energy and protein. Contrary to popular opinion, bread is not fattening but is an important part of a weight-maintaining or even weight-losing diet. The butter and spreads deliver far more calories than does the bread. In contrast to the bland taste of white bread, whole-grain breads have excellent flavours and do not need butter or jam to enhance your enjoyment.

I have included a number of bread and muffin recipes. Since you can buy excellent wholemeal breads, rye breads and pumpernickel at your local grocery or bakery, I have focused particularly on the oat breads that my family enjoys.

Wholemeal bread

Makes 1 × 450 g/1 lb loaf
Per serving: 99 KCal, 17.6 g carbohydrate, 3.2 g protein, 3.1 g fat, 0 mg cholesterol, 1.3 g fibre, 89 mg sodium

450 ml/16 fl oz skimmed milk   *5 ml/1 tsp salt*
2.5 ml/½ tsp sugar   *335 g/12 oz wholemeal flour*
10 ml/2 tsp dried yeast   *60 ml/2 fl oz vegetable oil*
335 g/12 oz plain strong white flour

Heat oven to 220°C/425°F/gas 7.

Heat milk to lukewarm, stir in sugar and sprinkle with yeast. Leave for 15 minutes.

Sift the plain flour and salt into a large bowl; add the wholemeal flour. Stir the oil into the yeast mixture. Pour on to the flours, mixing to make a soft dough. Add extra water if necessary. Knead for 5–10 minutes until smooth and elastic. Cover and leave to rise in a warm place for 30 minutes or until doubled in size. Gently knead the dough. Shape into a loaf and place on a greased baking sheet sprinkled with flour. Cover and leave to rise in a warm place for 30 minutes. Bake for 35–40 minutes or until bread sounds hollow when tapped on the bottom.

Oatmeal bread

Makes 2 × 450 g/1 lb loaves, 24 slices
Per serving: 129 KCal, 24.4 g carbohydrate, 4.8 g protein, 1.3 g fat, 0 mg cholesterol, 2.7 g fibre, 82 mg sodium

170 g/6 oz medium oatmeal	*15 g/½ oz margarine*
25 g/1 oz dried yeast	*2.5 ml/½ tsp salt*
225 ml/8 fl oz skimmed milk	*300 g/10½ oz wholemeal flour*
115 g/4 oz black treacle	*200 g/7 oz plain flour*

Heat oven to 180°C/350°F/gas 4.
   In a large mixing bowl pour 225 ml/8 fl oz boiling water over the oatmeal. Set aside to cool. Add the yeast to 115 ml/4 fl oz warm water. Leave for 15 minutes. Stir the milk, treacle, margarine, salt and yeast mixture into the oats. Beat in the flours. Knead for 5–10 minutes until well mixed. Return to an oiled bowl, turning dough to oil all sides. Cover and leave to rise until doubled in bulk. Knead again, divide dough in half and shape into two loaves. Place in oiled and floured 22 × 11.5 cm/8½ × 4½ in loaf tins. Leave to rise for 10 to 15 minutes. Bake for 1 hour. Remove from tins. Cool completely before slicing.

Bran muffins

Makes 12
Per serving: 111 KCal, 15.5 g carbohydrate, 3.7 g protein, 3.8 g fat, 1 mg cholesterol, 2.8 g fibre, 126 mg sodium

50 g/2 oz All-Bran	*50 g/2 oz sugar*
225 ml/8 fl oz skimmed milk	*egg replacer equivalent to 1 egg* or
50 g/2 oz wholemeal flour	*1 large egg white, lightly beaten*
75 g/3 oz plain flour	*45 ml/3 tbsp vegetable oil*
15 ml/1 tbsp baking powder	

Heat oven to 200°C/400°F/gas 6.
   Measure the All-Bran and milk into a large mixing bowl. Stir to mix. Stand for 1–2 minutes, until cereal is softened. Stir flours, baking powder and sugar together. Set aside. Add the egg replacer or white and oil to cereal and milk mixture. Beat well. Add flour mixture, stirring until just combined. Spoon batter evenly into 12 1 cm/½ in deep patty tins brushed with vegetable oil. Bake for 25 minutes, or until lightly browned.

Sour-dough starter

225 g/8 oz plain flour *1 packet active dry yeast*
10 ml/2 tsp sugar

Place ingredients in large porcelain bowl, add 575 ml/1 pint warm water, and mix well. Cover loosely and let stand in warm place for 2–4 days, stirring several times daily. Next, add 225 g/8 oz flour and 450 ml/16 fl oz water, and mix. Cover loosely and let stand for 12–24 hours for fermentation to begin. Remove amount needed for recipe and refrigerate. To reuse the starter, add more flour and water and repeat the process.

Sour-dough oat bread

Makes 2 × 450 g/1 lb loaves
Per serving: 112 KCal, 17.8 g carbohydrate, 4 g protein, 2.8 fat, 0 mg cholesterol, 2.7 g fibre, 1 mg sodium

25 g/1 oz dried yeast *115 g/4 oz sour-dough starter (see*
115 g/4 oz sugar *above)*
75 ml/3 fl oz vegetable oil *170 g/6 oz oat bran*
335 g/12 oz wholemeal flour

Heat oven to 170°C/325°F/gas 3.
Dissolve the yeast and sugar in 225 ml/8 fl oz warm water. Add the oil and sour-dough starter. Stir in the other dry ingredients, mix well and knead lightly. Divide the dough between two loaf tins, cover and put in a warm place to rise for about 1½ hours, or until doubled in size.
Bake for 35 minutes. Cover the tins with foil after 20 minutes.

Honey oatmeal bread

Makes 2 × 450 g/1 lb loaves, 24 slices
Per serving: 137 KCal, 25.4 g carbohydrate, 4.5 g protein, 1.9 g fat, 0 mg cholesterol, 1.9 g fibre, 112 mg sodium

75 g/3 oz rolled oats *25 g/1 oz margarine, melted*
25 g/1 oz dried yeast *200 g/7 oz wholemeal flour*
2.5 ml/½ tsp salt *300 g/10½ oz plain flour*
115 g/4 oz honey

Heat oven to 170°C/325°F/gas 3.
Pour 450 ml/16 fl oz boiling water over the rolled oats. Let it stand for 30 minutes. Soak the yeast in 75 ml/3 fl oz of lukewarm water for 15 minutes. Add the salt, honey and melted margarine to the oats. Stir in the yeast. Mix the flours together. Gradually add enough flour to make a soft dough. Knead for 5 to 10 minutes,

adding flour as needed, until smooth and elastic. Put the dough in an oiled bowl. Cover and leave in a warm place. When doubled in size, knead again, divide and put into 2 loaf tins. Bake for about 50 minutes.

Quick buttermilk rolls

Makes 12 to 15 rolls
Per serving: 117 KCal, 18.5 g carbohydrate, 3.7 g protein, 3.1 g fat, 0 mg cholesterol, 1.6 g fibre, 126 mg sodium

50 ml/2 fl oz warm water
15 g/½ oz dried yeast
170 ml/6 fl oz warm buttermilk (see note below)
2.5 ml/½ tsp bicarbonate of soda

25 g/1 oz sugar
2.5 ml/½ tsp salt
45 ml/3 tbsp vegetable oil
140 g/5 oz wholemeal flour
140 g/5 oz plain flour

Heat oven to 200°C/400°F/gas 6.
Mix all the ingredients together in a bowl. Shape into rolls and place on a greased baking sheet. Let rise for about 1 hour. Bake for 15 minutes.

NB   If buttermilk is unavailable make a similar product by adding 15 ml/1 tbsp vinegar or lemon juice to 225 ml/8 fl oz skimmed milk.

Oat muffins

Makes 12
Per serving: 110 KCal, 14.5 g carbohydrate, 4.4 g protein, 3.8 g fat, 1 mg cholesterol, 2.8 g fibre, 156 mg sodium

250 g/9 oz rolled oats
50 g/2 oz sugar
15 g/1 tbsp baking powder

335 ml/12 fl oz skimmed milk
2 egg whites
30 ml/2 tbsp vegetable oil

Heat oven to 200°C/400°F/gas 6.
Lightly grease 12 deep patty tins. Liquidize or blend the oats to a coarse flour. Mix together with the other dry ingredients. Combine milk, egg whites and oil and beat lightly. Add liquid to dry ingredients and stir until just blended. Pour into patty tins and bake for 20–25 minutes, or until lightly browned.

Oat bran muffins

Makes 10
Per serving: 90 KCal, 15.1 g carbohydrate, 5.4 g protein, 0.9 g fat, 0 mg cholesterol, 3.6 g fibre, 23 mg sodium

2 egg whites
225 ml/8 fl oz skimmed milk
75 g/3 oz apple sauce

115 g/4 oz oat bran
100 g/3½ oz self-raising flour
10 ml/2 tsp ground cinnamon

Heat oven to 200°C/400°F/gas 6.

Beat together egg whites and milk. Stir in the apple sauce. In a separate bowl mix together the dry ingredients. Mix the milk mixture into the dry ingredients until well blended – do not beat. Brush deep non-stick patty tins with vegetable oil. Pour the mixture into the prepared tins and bake for 15 minutes.

Cornmeal muffins

Makes 12
Per serving: 115 KCal, 15.4 g carbohydrate, 3.5 g protein, 4.4 g fat, 0 mg cholesterol, 1.8 g fibre, 187 mg sodium

45 ml/3 tbsp vegetable oil
100 g/3½ oz wholemeal flour
115 g/4 oz yellow cornmeal
50 g/2 oz sugar
20 ml/4 tsp baking powder

5 ml/1 tsp bicarbonate of soda
225 ml/8 fl oz skimmed milk
egg replacer equivalent to 1 egg or
1 large egg white, lightly beaten

Heat oven to 220°C/425°F/gas 7.

Brush 12 6.5 cm/2½ in deep patty tins with vegetable oil and set aside. Mix dry ingredients together in a bowl. Mix together the milk, egg replacer or white and oil. Add to dry ingredients all at once, stirring only until just blended. Do not overmix. Spoon batter into prepared tins, filling each three-quarters full. Bake for 20–25 minutes. Remove immediately and cool on a wire rack. Serve warm.

Oat bran raisin muffins See photograph, page 44

Makes 10
Per serving: 112 KCal, 12.2 g carbohydrate, 6.9 g protein, 3.9 g fat, 0 mg cholesterol, 6.1 g fibre, 189 mg sodium

225 g/8 oz oat bran
2.5 ml/½ tsp artificial sweetener
50 g/2 oz raisins
15 ml/1 tbsp baking powder
5 ml/1 tsp each ground cinnamon,

nutmeg and ginger (optional)
170 ml/6 fl oz skimmed milk
egg replacer equivalent to 1 egg or
1 large egg white, lightly beaten
15 ml/1 tbsp vegetable oil

Heat oven to 220°C/425°F/gas 7.

Grease the bases of 10 medium sized patty tins or line with paper cases. Mix together the dry ingredients. Add the milk, egg replacer or white and oil, and mix until the dry ingredients are just moistened. Fill the prepared tins three-quarters full. Bake for about 15 minutes or until golden brown.

Wholemeal muffins

Makes 12
Per serving: 103 KCal, 13.3 g carbohydrate, 5 g protein, 3.3 g fat,
1 mg cholesterol, 3.3 g fibre, 132 mg sodium

335 ml/12 fl oz skimmed milk   *20 ml/4 tsp vegetable oil*
50 g/2 oz oat bran   *75 g/3 oz rolled oats*
egg replacer equivalent to 1 egg or   *100 g/3½ oz wholemeal flour*
 1 large egg white, lightly beaten   *15 ml/1 tbsp baking powder*
25 g/1 oz artificial sweetener

Heat oven to 200°C/400°F/gas 6.
   Coat 12 deep non-stick patty tins with vegetable oil or use paper
cases. In a bowl, mix together the milk and oat bran. Add the egg
replacer or white, artificial sweetener and oil and mix well. Add
the remaining ingredients to the oat mixture, mixing until
ingredients are evenly blended. Fill the prepared patty tins ⅔ full.
Bake for about 20 minutes or until light golden brown.

Blackberry muffins

Makes 12
Per serving: 107 KCal, 12.8 g carbohydrate, 4.1 g protein, 4 g fat,
0 mg cholesterol, 2.2 g fibre, 134 mg sodium

100 g/3½ oz wholemeal flour   *egg replacer equivalent to 1 egg* or
75 g/3 oz rolled oats   *1 large egg white, lightly beaten*
2.5 ml/½ tsp ground cinnamon   *30 ml/2 tbsp oil*
15 ml/1 tbsp baking powder   *140 g/5 oz blackberries*
170 ml/6 fl oz skimmed milk

Heat oven to 200°C/400°F/gas 6.
   Mix together the wholemeal flour, rolled oats, cinnamon and
baking powder. Whisk together the skimmed milk, egg replacer
or white and oil. Stir into the dry ingredients until evenly blended.
Add the blackberries. Bake in deep, non-stick patty tins or paper
cases for 20 minutes or until lightly brown.

Oat spice biscuits

Makes 36
Per serving: 72 KCal, 9.3 g carbohydrate, 1.3 g protein, 3.3 g fat,
0 mg cholesterol, 1 g fibre, 27 mg sodium   ➡

Oat bran raisin muffins (*top*, see page 43), Blackberry muffins (*centre*),
Oat spice biscuits (*bottom*)

250 g/9 oz packet spiced cake mix
115 g/4 oz rolled oats
170 g/6 oz raisins
50 g/2 oz nuts, finely chopped
50 g/2 oz wholemeal flour
50 ml/2 fl oz vegetable oil

egg replacer equivalent to 1 egg or
    1 large egg white, lightly beaten
25 g/1 oz dark brown sugar
5 ml/1 tsp instant coffee powder
2.5 ml/½ tsp vanilla essence

Heat oven to 190°C/375°F/gas 5.

Mix together all the ingredients in a large mixing bowl. Drop teaspoonfuls of the mixture on to a baking sheet. Bake for 10 minutes or until edges are brown. Cool on a wire rack.

Oatmeal biscuits

Makes 24
Per serving: 71 KCal, 7.1 g carbohydrate, 1.6 g protein, 4 g fat, 0 mg cholesterol, 0.7 fibre, 69 mg sodium

75 g/3 oz plain flour
2.5 ml/½ tsp ground cinnamon
50 g/2 oz light soft brown sugar
50 g/2 oz margarine, softened
2.5 ml/½ tsp vanilla essence
2.5 ml/½ tsp baking powder

2.5 ml/½ tsp bicarbonate of soda
1.25 ml/¼ tsp salt
egg replacer equivalent to 1 egg or
    1 large egg white, lightly beaten
50 g/2 oz walnuts, chopped
75 g/3 oz rolled oats

Heat oven to 190°C/375°F/gas 5.

In a large bowl, beat together the flour and next seven ingredients. Stir in the egg replacer or white, chopped walnuts and oats. Drop tablespoons of the mixture about 5 cm/2 in apart on to baking sheets. Bake for 10 minutes or until well browned around the edges (centres will be lighter). Cool on a wire rack. Store any leftover biscuits in an airtight tin.

Banana bread

Makes 1 × 900 g/2 lb loaf, 20 slices
Per serving: 92 KCal, 16.8 g carbohydrate, 3.6 g protein, 1.1 g fat, 0 mg cholesterol, 1.8 g fibre, 87 mg sodium

egg replacer equivalent to 2 eggs or
    2 large egg whites
75 g/3 oz sugar
115 g/4 oz cottage cheese, sieved
115 ml/4 fl oz honey
5 ml/1 tsp vanilla essence
2 over-ripe bananas, mashed

15 ml/1 tbsp oil
225 g/8 oz wholemeal flour
7.5 ml/1½ tsp baking powder
5 ml/1 tsp bicarbonate of soda
2.5 ml/½ tsp ground cinnamon
    (optional)
15 ml/1 tsp skimmed milk

Heat oven to 180°C/350°F/gas 4.

Beat the egg replacer or whites into the sugar, sieved cottage cheese, honey and vanilla essence. Add the bananas and oil and mix together. Sift the flour, baking powder, bicarbonate of soda and cinnamon. Combine the egg and flour mixtures and milk and stir until just blended. Pour into a greased 900 g/2 lb loaf tin. Bake for 1–1¼ hours. Cool in the tin for about 10 minutes before removing to a wire rack.

SOUPS

On a cold winter day, there's nothing like a bowl of hot soup. Whether as a preliminary or the main event, soups are nutritious and economical. Homemade soups are tastier and have less fat and salt than commercial ones. If you are short on time you may prepare the soup one evening, refrigerate it and finish it the next evening. Soups are a great place to use leftovers. Also, most soups can be frozen or used with other ingredients. We use bean and lentil soups and chilli to add greater variety to the bean dishes.

Asparagus soup
See photograph, page 48

Serves 2
Per serving: 128 KCal, 13.5 g carbohydrate, 7 g protein, 5.1 g fat, 2 mg cholesterol, 2.5 g fibre, 375 mg sodium

225 g/8 oz cooked asparagus　　*225 ml/8 fl oz skimmed milk*
1 packet onion soup mix

Drain the asparagus and chop or purée in the blender. Combine in a saucepan with the skimmed milk and onion soup mix. Simmer for 15 minutes.

Gazpacho

Serves 8
Per serving: 52 KCal, 10.2 g carbohydrate, 2.1 g protein, 0.3 g fat, 0 mg cholesterol, 2.9 g fibre, 135 mg sodium

6 ripe tomatoes, peeled and chopped　　*1 stick celery, chopped*
1 small onion, chopped　　*50 g/2 oz lemon juice*
½ green pepper, chopped　　*8–10 drops tabasco sauce*
50 g/2 oz cucumber, chopped　　*ice cubes*
575 ml/1 pint tomato juice

Place all the ingredients in a liquidizer or blender goblet and blend until smooth. For a coarser soup, use the food processor for chopping. Chill in the refrigerator for at least 3 hours. Serve cold, adding a few ice cubes to the serving bowl if liked.

Vegetable barley soup

Serves 4
Per serving: 130 KCal, 25.2 g carbohydrate, 4.7 g protein, 1.2 g fat, 0 mg cholesterol, 5 g fibre, 431 mg sodium

140 ml/5 fl oz condensed onion soup
5 ml/1 tsp dried oregano
pinch of pepper
50 g/2 oz carrots, sliced
50 g/2 oz celery, sliced

75 g/3 oz shredded cabbage
225 g/8 oz tinned tomatoes
140 g/5 oz frozen cut green beans
115 g/4 oz quick cooking barley

In saucepan combine 0.7 l/1¼ pints water with the onion soup, oregano and pepper. Bring to the boil. Add the vegetables and barley. Simmer, covered, for 30 minutes.

Split pea soup

Serves 6
Per serving: 182 KCal, 31.5 g carbohydrate, 12.6 g protein, 0.6 g fat, 0 mg cholesterol, 7.6 g fibre, 319 mg sodium

335 g/12 oz dried green split peas
½ green pepper, chopped
1 stick celery, chopped
115 g/4 oz potatoes, diced

50 g/2 oz onion, chopped
1 carrot, grated
1.25 ml/¼ tsp marjoram
1.25 ml/½ tsp salt

Simmer the peas and green pepper in 1¼ l/2½ pints water for 1¼ hours. Add all the remaining vegetables and seasonings and simmer until tender, about 45 minutes.

Garden vegetable soup

Serves 6
Per serving: 97 KCal, 18.7 g carbohydrate, 4.4 g protein, 0.5 g fat, 0 mg cholesterol, 6.7 g fibre, 463 mg sodium

1 beef stock cube
450 ml/16 fl oz tomato juice

2 medium potatoes, diced
2 medium carrots, diced

Asparagus soup (*top*, see page 47), Split pea soup (*centre*), Vegetable barley soup (*bottom*)

75 g/3 oz green beans, diced
1 medium onion, diced
1 medium courgette, diced
2 sticks celery, diced

3 medium tomatoes, diced
½ green pepper, diced
1.25 ml/¼ tsp basil
1.25 ml/¼ tsp marjoram

Dissolve the beef stock cubes in the tomato juice combined with 700 ml/1¼ pints water. Add the vegetables and seasonings. Bring to the boil. Simmer until the vegetables are cooked. Serve hot.

Cream of potato soup

Serves 8
Per serving: 116 KCal, 21.8 g carbohydrate, 6.3 g protein, 0.4 g fat, 2 mg cholesterol, 3.0 g fibre, 158 mg sodium

6 medium potatoes, peeled and sliced
2 medium onions, chopped
2 sticks celery, diced
2.5 ml/½ tsp salt

875 ml/1½ pints skimmed milk, scalded
2.5 ml/½ tsp pepper
15 ml/1 tbsp chopped parsley

Place the vegetables, salt and 700 ml/1¼ pints water in a large saucepan and cook until tender. Mash the vegetables, add the scalded milk and pepper. Serve hot, garnished with parsley.

Lentil soup

Serves 6
Per serving: 203 KCal, 31.8 g carbohydrate, 17.1 g protein, 0.8 g fat, 0 mg cholesterol, 12.6 g fibre, 251 mg sodium

450 g/1 lb Continental lentils, soaked
and drained (see page 76)
115 g/4 oz onion, sliced
1 clove garlic

1 stick celery, sliced
2 carrots, thinly sliced
1 bay leaf
15 ml/1 tbsp soy sauce (low-salt)

Place the lentils, onion and garlic in a large saucepan with 1½ l/2¾ pints of water and bring to the boil. Lower heat and simmer for 1 hour or until the lentils are soft. Add the celery, carrots and seasonings and simmer until the vegetables are tender, about 30 minutes. Remove the bay leaf and serve hot.

Bean soup

Serves 6
Per serving: 77 KCal, 11.5 g carbohydrate, 6.5 g protein, 0.6 g fat, 0 mg cholesterol, 7.7 g fibre, 349 mg sodium

450 g/1 lb haricot or other dried beans,
soaked, drained and rinsed (see
page 76)

½ green pepper, chopped
115 g/4 oz onion, chopped
2.5 ml/½ tsp seasoning salt

10 ml/2 tsp chicken stock	*1 carrot*
1 bay leaf	*1 stick celery*

In a large saucepan place the beans, green pepper, half the onion, salt, chicken stock, 3 1/5 pints water and the bay leaf. Bring to the boil, then simmer for 2½ hours. Add the diced carrot, celery and remaining onion. Cook for 30 minutes. Remove the bay leaf and serve.

Chilli

Serves 6
Per serving: 214 KCal, 36.3 g carbohydrate, 9.2 g protein, 3.6 g fat, 0 mg cholesterol, 10.8 g fibre, 432 mg sodium

170 g/6 oz onion, chopped	*225 ml/8 oz beef stock*
1 green pepper, chopped	*15 ml/1 tbsp chilli powder, or*
1 clove garlic, crushed	*according to taste*
15 ml/1 tbsp oil	*450 g/1 lb tinned red kidney beans,*
785 g/1 lb 12 oz tinned tomatoes	*drained*
335 g/12 oz sweetcorn kernels	*2.5 ml/½ tsp ground cumin*
115 g/4 oz tomato purée, mixed with	*1.25 ml/¼ tsp pepper*
its own volume of water	

Brown the onion, pepper and garlic in the oil. Add the rest of the ingredients and bring to the boil, cover and simmer for 1 hour or until the flavour has mellowed and the sauce has thickened. Serve over rice if desired.

APPETIZERS, SNACKS AND SANDWICHES

A good appetizer will tease your appetite, not drown it. A chilled glass of tomato or vegetable juice is just right to wake up your taste buds. To socialize before dinner, nibble on raw vegetables with a small amount of tangy dip. The calorie-conscious person, and aren't we all, avoids high-fat items such as cream cheese, cock-

OVERLEAF: Spiced drumsticks (*top right*, see page 54), Curry vegetable dip (*top left*, see page 55), Vegetarian sandwich filling (*bottom right*, see page 55), Pitta bread sandwiches (*bottom left*, see page 55)

tail biscuits, pastries and titbits fried in batter. This section gives you a few suggestions for appetizers and the vegetable section (page 66) directs you to many tasty fresh vegetables.

Eating light snacks is an excellent practice. People who eat six snacks daily, nibblers, are healthier than those who have only one or two meals daily, gorgers. Eating the right sort of snacks and in moderation will serve you well; having part of your lunch (a slice of bread, part of a sandwich or fruit) at midmorning and part of your dinner mid-afternoon will give you additional benefits. However, you should avoid unscheduled snacks of high-calorie foods such as sweets, nuts and potato crisps. The meal plan gives you many suggestions; I find that cereal makes a fine evening snack.

Lunching away from home can wreck your diet plan. Restaurants, snack shops or vending machines may not have what you need, so I recommend that you plan ahead and carry your lunch with you. Look at the basic meal plan for 1500 calories (page 25). You could take a small can of tomato juice, a salad in a plastic container, a sandwich, several fresh vegetables (carrots, celery and radishes) and fruit. A person of habit like me has the same thing for lunch every day – a large can of vegetable juice, two oat bran muffins and fruit. With a little experience you can take an interesting lunch or select salads, soups, vegetables and fruit for a tasty lunch in a restaurant.

Tomato juice cocktail

Serves 12
Per serving: 33 KCal, 6.7 g carbohydrate, 1.1 g protein, 0.2 g fat, 0 mg cholesterol, 1.3 g fibre, 234 mg sodium

1.3 l/2¼ pints tomato juice   *50 ml/2 fl oz lemon juice*
15 ml/1 tbsp Worcestershire sauce   *1 vegetable stock cube (optional)*
dash of tabasco sauce

Blend all the ingredients together and chill well before serving.

Spiced drumsticks   See photograph, page 52

Serves 4
Per serving: 129 KCal, 5.3 g carbohydrate, 13.3 g protein, 6.1 g fat, 35 mg cholesterol, 1.1 g fibre, 352 mg sodium

15 ml/1 tbsp wholemeal flour   *25 g/1 oz rolled oats*
5 ml/1 tsp salt (optional)   *grated rind of 1 orange*
egg replacer equivalent to 1 egg or *10 ml/2 tsp curry powder*
  1 large egg white, lightly beaten   *4 chicken drumsticks*

Heat oven to 180°C/350°F/gas 4.
Mix the flour and salt, if using, together on one plate. Beat the egg replacer or egg white lightly with 15 ml/1 tbsp water in a shallow

dish. Mix oats, orange rind and curry powder on another plate. Coat the drumsticks first with flour, then egg replacer or egg white, then oat mixture. Pat oats firmly on to drumsticks to coat evenly. Cook on top shelf of oven for 20 minutes, then increase temperature to 220°C/425°F/gas 7 and cook for another 15 minutes until crisp. Serve hot or cold.

An alternative This coating can be used for fish.

Pitta bread sandwiches   See photograph, page 52

Serves 4
Per serving: 204 KCal, 27.3 g carbohydrate, 15.8 g protein, 3.5 g fat, 19 mg cholesterol, 4.3 g fibre, 438 mg sodium

1 tomato, finely chopped
¼ cucumber, diced
4 large mushrooms, sliced
8 lettuce leaves
2 spring onions, sliced
75 g/3 oz cooked turkey, ham or beef,

cut into thin shreds, 2.5 cm/1 in long
50 g/2 oz low-fat cheese, cut into 0.5 cm/¼ in cubes
4 large pittas
60 ml/4 tbsp French dressing (see page 64)

Arrange the prepared vegetables, meat and cheese on plates. Cut the pitta bread in halves (to make two pouches each). Let each person fill his or her own pouches. Use dressing as desired.

Vegetarian sandwich filling

Serves 4   See photograph, page 52
Per serving: 62 KCal, 9.4 g carbohydrate, 2.1 g protein, 1.8 g fat, 2 mg cholesterol, 3.3 g fibre, 377 mg sodium

75 g/3 oz fresh tomato, diced
50 g/2 oz onion, diced
75 g/3 oz fresh broccoli, diced
75 g/3 oz fresh carrots, diced
75 g/3 oz fresh cauliflower, diced
75 g/3 oz tinned sweetcorn kernels, drained

2.5 ml/½ tsp dill weed
2.5 ml/½ tsp dried oregano
2.5 ml/½ tsp salt (optional)
60 ml/2 fl oz Thousand Island dressing (see page 64)

Mix the vegetables, herbs, salt and salad dressing together. Cover and chill. Use as sandwich filling or a salad.

Curry vegetable dip   See photograph, page 52

Serves 8
Per serving: 9 KCal, 1.3 g carbohydrate, 0.9 g protein, 0 g fat, 0 mg cholesterol, 0 g fibre, 35 mg sodium

115 ml/4 fl oz low-fat plain yoghurt
1.25 ml/¼ tsp curry powder
1.25 ml/¼ tsp lemon juice

pinch ground cumin
pinch white pepper

Mix together all the ingredients in small bowl and chill. Serve as a dip with assorted fresh raw vegetables.

Mexicali bean dip

Makes 575 g/1 lb 3 oz; 15 ml/1 tbsp per serving
Per serving: 19 KCal, 3.4 g carbohydrate, 1 g protein, 0.2 g fat, 0 mg cholesterol, 1.1 g fibre, 80 mg sodium

450 g/1 lb tin baked beans
75 g/3 oz cooked chick peas (see page 76)
30 ml/2 tbsp taco sauce

15 ml/1 tbsp dried onion
5 ml/1 tsp chilli powder
corn chips or *assorted fresh raw vegetables*

In a medium bowl, mash together the beans and chick peas with a fork; stir in all the remaining ingredients except the corn chips. Cover and refrigerate for about 2 hours. Serve as a dip with corn chips or assorted fresh raw vegetables.

Vegetable spread

Makes about 450 g/1 lb; 30 ml/2 tbsp per serving
Per serving: 7 KCal, 0.7 g carbohydrate, 0.8 g protein, 0.1 g fat, 0 mg cholesterol, 0.3 g fibre, 23 mg sodium

1 stick celery, chopped
50 g/2 oz cucumber, chopped
75 g/3 oz green pepper, chopped
140 g/5 oz tomato, chopped

30 ml/2 tbsp onion, chopped
30 ml/2 tbsp dill pickle, chopped
75 g/3 oz cottage cheese, sieved
1.25 ml/¼ tsp seasoning salt (optional)

For a coarse spread, mix all the ingredients together. For a soft, creamy spread, place the mixture in a blender goblet or food processor and blend until smooth. Chill. Serve as dip with fresh raw vegetables, or spread on crispbread.

Cucumber and cheese spread

Makes about 400 g/14 oz; 15 ml/1 tbsp per serving
Per serving: 11 KCal, 0.6 g carbohydrate, 1.8 g protein, 0.2 g fat, 1 mg cholesterol, 0.1 g fibre, 42 mg sodium

225 g/8 oz cottage cheese, sieved
5 ml/1 tsp lemon juice
dash of tabasco sauce
5 ml/1 tsp grated onion

170 g/6 oz cucumber, finely chopped
1.25 ml/¼ tsp grated horseradish (optional)

Mix all the ingredients together, cover and chill for at least 1 hour. Makes a soft spread.

Carrot-pineapple salad (*top*, see page 59), Oriental garden salad (*centre*, see page 58), Spinach salad (*bottom*, see page 58)

SALADS AND DRESSINGS

I love salads. Start with lettuce, spinach or your favourite greens. Add sliced or cubed cucumber, spring onions, mushrooms and tomatoes. Sprinkle on a crunchy oat topping. Top with bean or alfalfa sprouts and then add a low-calorie dressing. This colourful dish has vitamins, minerals and fibre but very few calories.

The secret to enjoying tasty and filling but low-calorie salads is in the dressing. Shop around or experiment until you find your favourite dressing with a low-fat content. On pages 64–5 I have given you a few ideas for low-fat dressings.

Oriental garden salad   See photograph, page 57

Serves 6
Per serving: 84 KCal, 7.6 g carbohydrate, 2.5 g protein, 4.8 g fat, 0 mg cholesterol, 3.8 g fibre, 329 mg sodium

170 g/6 oz fresh mangetout peas
30 ml/2 tbsp salad oil
75 ml/3 fl oz red wine vinegar
10 ml/2 tsp sugar
15 ml/1 tbsp soy sauce

1.25 ml/¼ tsp ground ginger
170 g/6 oz Chinese leaves, chopped
225 g/8 oz lettuce, shredded
200 g/7 oz beansprouts
2 tomatoes, chopped

Cook the mangetout peas in 575 ml/1 pint lightly salted boiling water for 1 minute and drain. Place oil, vinegar, sugar, soy sauce and ginger in a liquidizer or blender goblet and blend until smooth. Pour dressing over peas, cover and marinate for 2–3 hours in the refrigerator. Just before serving add the remaining ingredients to the marinated peas. Toss well.

Spinach salad   See photograph, page 57

Serves 8
Per serving: 54 KCal, 2.2 g carbohydrate, 0.9 g protein, 4.6 g fat, 0 mg cholesterol, 1.0 g fibre, 12 mg sodium

1 clove garlic, crushed
50 ml/2 fl oz vegetable oil
115 g/4 oz raw spinach, shredded
50 g/2 oz spring onion, chopped
280 g/10 oz tomatoes, chopped
50 g/2 oz mushrooms, sliced

5 ml/1 tsp oregano
1.25 ml/¼ tsp pepper
15 ml/1 tbsp wine vinegar
15 ml/1 tbsp lemon juice
1.25 ml/¼ tsp dry mustard

Stir the garlic into the oil, marinate for 1 hour. Place the spinach, onion, tomatoes and mushrooms in a salad bowl. Mix together the remaining ingredients with the garlic oil. Pour on to the salad mixture and toss well.

Coleslaw

Serves 6
Per serving: 48 KCal, 8.3 g carbohydrate, 2.7 g protein, 0.4 g fat, 1 mg cholesterol, 3.4 g fibre, 129 mg sodium

75 g/3 oz red cabbage, shredded
170 g/6 oz green cabbage, shredded
4 medium carrots, grated

Dressing:
5 ml/1 tsp celery seed
115 ml/4 fl oz low-fat plain yoghurt
5 ml/1 tsp dry English mustard
15 ml/1 tbsp cider vinegar
5 ml/1 tsp sugar

Mix together the vegetables. Whisk the dressing ingredients and combine with the vegetables. Cover and chill before serving.

Carrot-pineapple salad   See photograph, page 57

Serves 4
Per serving: 65 KCal, 14.6 g carbohydrate, 1.5 g protein, 0.1 g fat, 0 mg cholesterol, 2.1 g fibre, 31 mg sodium

1 carrot, finely grated
1 apple, finely grated
140 g/5 oz unsweetened pineapple
  chunks

50 g/2 oz raisins
15 ml/1 tbsp low-fat plain yoghurt
pinch of cinnamon
2.5 ml/¼ tsp artificial sweetener

Mix the first 4 ingredients together. Combine the yoghurt, cinnamon and artificial sweetener. Pour over fruit. Mix thoroughly and chill.

Mexican fruit salad   See photograph, page 60

Serves 10
Per serving: 131 KCal, 29.8 g carbohydrate, 2.0 g protein, 0.4 g fat, 0 mg cholesterol, 5.0 g fibre, 40 mg sodium

450 g/1 lb apples, diced (unpeeled)
4 oranges, peeled and segmented
4 bananas, sliced
560 g/1 lb 4 oz pineapple pieces or

chunks, tinned in own juice
15 ml/1 tbsp lime juice
450 g/1 lb sliced beetroot, drained
lettuce leaves

OVERLEAF: Pickle-pea salad (*centre top*, see page 62), Rice-fruit salad (*centre right*, see page 62), Mexican fruit salad (*centre left*, see page 59), German hot potato salad (*bottom right*, see page 63), Bean salad (*bottom left*, see page 62)

Toss together the apples, oranges and bananas, drain the pineapple and add with the lime juice. Chill. Just before serving, add the well-drained beetroot. Serve on a bed of lettuce.

Rice-fruit salad
See photograph, page 60

Serves 6
Per serving: 138 KCal, 30.3 g carbohydrate, 3.5 g protein, 0.3 g fat, 0 mg cholesterol, 2.6 g fibre, 68 mg sodium

500 g/1 lb 2 oz cooked rice, cooled
700 g/1½ lb satsumas, peeled and segmented
2 sticks celery, sliced diagonally

235 g/8½ oz tin crushed pineapple (in own juice)
115 ml/4 fl oz low-fat plain yoghurt
lettuce leaves

Blend all the ingredients together and chill. Serve on a bed of shredded lettuce.

Pickle-pea salad
See photograph, page 60

Serves 2
Per serving: 115 KCal, 15.3 g carbohydrate, 10 g protein, 1.5 g fat, 1 mg cholesterol, 3.7 g fibre, 497 mg sodium

115 g/4 oz cooked, drained peas
25 g/1 oz low-fat cheese, grated
25 g/1 oz dill pickle, grated
15 ml/1 tbsp diced pimiento
15 ml/1 tbsp chopped onion
pinch of pepper

50 ml/2 fl oz low-fat plain yoghurt

Garnish:
4 slices tomato
lettuce leaves

Combine all the ingredients. Cover and chill 3 – 4 hours. Serve on tomato slices with lettuce.

Bean salad
See photograph, page 60

Serves 8
Per serving: 164 KCal, 25.9 g carbohydrate, 5.8 g protein, 4.1 g fat, 0 mg cholesterol, 9.5 g fibre, 144 mg sodium

10 ml/2 tsp sugar
30 ml/2 tbsp salad oil
115 ml/4 fl oz cider vinegar
700 g/1½ lb French beans, cooked

450 g/1 lb tinned red kidney beans, rinsed and drained
450 g/1 lb tinned sweetcorn, drained
50 g/2 oz onion, chopped
25 g/1 oz red pepper, chopped

Blend together the sugar, oil and vinegar. Place the vegetables in a serving bowl. Pour over the dressing. Cover and refrigerate overnight.

Potato salad

Serves 6
Per serving: 72 KCal, 14.6 g carbohydrate, 2.6 g protein, 0.4 g fat,
0 mg cholesterol, 2.5 g fibre, 153 mg sodium

50 g/2 oz dill pickles, finely chopped
450 g/1 lb cooked potatoes, diced
½ green pepper, chopped
1 stick celery, chopped
30 g/2 tbsp onions, chopped

1 carrot, grated
5 ml/1 tsp celery seed
5 ml/1 tsp cider vinegar
5 ml/1 tsp dry mustard
75 ml/3 fl oz low-fat plain yoghurt

Mix together the first 6 ingredients. Combine the last 4
ingredients, pour over the vegetables and toss. Chill for several
hours before serving.

German hot potato salad

Serves 6 See photograph, page 60
Per serving: 105 KCal, 18.9 g carbohydrate, 2.9 g protein, 2.0 g fat,
0 mg cholesterol, 2.6 g fibre, 313 mg sodium

115 g/4 oz onion, chopped
5 ml/1 tsp sugar
2.5 ml/½ tsp salt
5 ml/1 tsp wholemeal flour
1.25 ml/¼ tsp pepper

45 ml/3 tbsp red wine vinegar
6 potatoes, cooked and sliced
50 g/2 oz bacon, crisply grilled and chopped

In a medium frying pan cook the onion in 115 ml/4 fl oz water
until translucent. Stir in the sugar, salt, flour and pepper. Add the
vinegar and cook until slightly thickened. Gently stir in the
potatoes and chopped bacon. Serve hot.

Italian bean salad

Serves 3
Per serving: 208 KCal, 32 g carbohydrate, 12.6 g protein, 3.3 g fat, 1
mg cholesterol, 10.8 g fibre, 252 mg sodium

450 g/1 lb tin baked beans, rinsed and drained
50 g/2 oz mozzarella cheese, cubed
50 g/2 oz carrot, sliced
50 g/2 oz courgettes, cut into strips
50 g/2 oz green pepper, diced
30 ml/2 tbsp Zero salad dressing (see page 64)

1.25 ml/¼ tsp dried oregano

Garnish:
salad greens
tomato wedges
parsley

In a bowl, mix together all the ingredients except the greens. Chill
for at least 4 hours. Serve on salad greens, garnished with tomato
wedges and parsley.

Zero salad dressing

Makes about 575 ml/1 pint; 15 ml/1 tbsp per serving
Per serving: 3 KCal, 0.7 g carbohydrate, 0.1 g protein, 0 g fat, 0 mg cholesterol, 0.2 g fibre, 16 mg sodium

8 g/1½ tsp green pepper, minced   *200 ml/7 fl oz vinegar*
8 g/1½ tsp onion, minced   *275 ml/10 fl oz tomato juice*
75 g/3 oz carrots, minced   *artificial sweetener (optional)*

Mix all the ingredients in a 1 1/2 pint jar and store in the refrigerator. Shake before using.

French dressing

Makes about 575 ml/1 pint; 15 ml/1 tbsp per serving
Per serving: 8 KCal, 0.5 g carbohydrate, 1.3 g protein, 0.1 g fat, 0 mg cholesterol, 0 g fibre, 50 mg sodium

170 g/6 oz cottage cheese, sieved   *5 ml/1 tsp Worcestershire sauce*
65 ml/2½ fl oz tomato juice   *1.25 ml/¼ tsp onion salt*
2.5 ml/½ tsp mixed dried herbs

Blend all the ingredients until smooth. Serve over green salad.

Creamed herb dressing

Makes about 20 servings; 15 ml/1 tbsp per serving
Per serving: 9 KCal, 1.4 g carbohydrate, 0.8 g protein, 0 g fat, 0 mg cholesterol, 0 g fibre, 32 mg sodium

225 g/8 fl oz low-fat plain yoghurt   *5 ml/1 tsp mixed dried herbs*
30 ml/2 tbsp chives, chopped   *15 ml/1 tbsp lemon juice*
5 ml/1 tsp chopped dill

Place all the ingredients in a blender and blend until smooth. Cover and refrigerate overnight. Best served with green salads.

Thousand Island dressing

Makes about 28 servings; 15 ml/1 tbsp per serving
Per serving: 10 KCal, 1.6 g carbohydrate, 0.4 g protein, 0.2 g fat, 0 mg cholesterol, 0 g fibre, 80 mg sodium

275 ml/10 fl oz tin tomato soup   *30 ml/2 tbsp green pepper, chopped*
45 ml/3 tbsp cottage cheese, sieved   *5 ml/1 tsp dry mustard*
30 ml/2 tbsp dill pickles, chopped   *10 ml/2 tsp onion, chopped*

Place all the ingredients in a blender. Purée until smooth. Chill before serving.

Fruit salad dressing

Makes about 250 ml/½ pint; 15 ml/1 tbsp per serving
Per serving: 8 KCal, 2.0 g carbohydrate, 0.1 g protein, 0.1 g fat,
0 mg cholesterol, 0 g fibre, 0 mg sodium

45 ml/3 tbsp commercial fruit pectin
(eg, Certo)
225 ml/8 fl oz unsweetened pine-
apple juice

5 ml/1 tsp poppy seeds
15 ml/1 tbsp lemon juice

Purée all the ingredients in a blender. Cover and chill before serving over fresh fruit.

VEGETABLES

My favourite Sunday lunch is a spinach salad, four different vegetables, a bran muffin and a baked apple – I get these at a nearby
cafeteria after church. Following the HCF diet over the past seven
years has made me a connoisseur of vegetables. I like them lightly
steamed or boiled and flavoured with herbs or spices.

I have included some ideas for flavouring vegetables in the
recipes and you can also develop your own flavouring techniques
using different herbs and spices.

Since vegetables are rich in fibre, vitamins and minerals while
low in calories, we include generous helpings at all meals, and
for snacks.

Raw vegetables
Fresh raw vegetables make excellent snacks or low-calorie appetizers. Serve them with one of the low-calorie vegetable dips (pages 55–6). These raw vegetables average less than 10 calories per 50 g/2 oz; you can have 50 g/2 oz–115 g/4 oz per meal:

asparagus spears	cucumber slices
broccoli florets	green beans
carrot sticks	green pepper strips
cauliflower florets	mushrooms
celery sticks	radish roses
cherry tomatoes	spring onions
courgette sticks	turnip wedges

Cooked vegetables
Steamed or cooked without fat, 75 g/3 oz of these vegetables average only 20 calories:

asparagus	cucumber
aubergine	green beans
beetroot	green pepper
broccoli	greens – kale, spinach, spring
Brussels sprouts	marrow
cabbage	mushrooms
carrots	okra (ladies' fingers)
cauliflower	onions
celery	tomatoes
courgettes	turnips

Asparagus delight

Serves 6
Per serving: 36 KCal, 4.8 g carbohydrate, 3.4 g protein, 0.3 g fat, 0 mg cholesterol, 2.6 g fibre, 108 mg sodium

1 stick celery, chopped
½ green pepper, chopped
1 small onion, diced
2.5 ml/½ tsp salt (optional)

550 g/1 lb 4 oz fresh or frozen
  asparagus spears
paprika pepper

Place celery, green pepper, onion, salt, if using, and 115 ml/4 fl oz water in a saucepan, cover and cook for about 5 minutes until vegetables are just tender. Add the asparagus and steam for 12–15 minutes. Place in a warmed serving dish and sprinkle with paprika pepper.

Creamed beetroot

Serves 6
Per serving: 36 KCal, 6.7 g carbohydrate, 2.1 g protein, 0.1 g fat,
0 mg cholesterol, 1.4 g fibre, 190 mg sodium

115 ml/4 fl oz low-fat plain yoghurt   *1.25 ml/¼ tsp pepper*
5 ml/1 tsp Dijon mustard   *450 g/1 lb cooked beetroot, diced*
5 ml/1 tsp lemon juice

Blend together the yoghurt, mustard, lemon juice and pepper.
Add the cooked beetroot and stir carefully. Serve hot or
chilled.

Quickly pickled beetroot

Serves 2
Per serving: 60 KCal, 12.5 g carbohydrate, 2 g protein, 0.2 g fat,
0 mg cholesterol, 3.4 g fibre, 284 mg sodium

225 g/8 oz tinned beetroot, sliced   *1.25 ml/¼ tsp ground allspice*
60 ml/2 fl oz vinegar   *pinch of salt*
2.5 ml/½ tsp artificial sweetener   *½ medium onion, sliced and separated*
1.25 ml/¼ tsp ground ginger   *into rings (optional)*

Drain the beetroot, reserving 115 ml/4 fl oz liquid. In a saucepan
combine the beetroot liquid with the next 5 ingredients. Bring to
the boil, then pour over the beetroot. Refrigerate overnight in a
covered bowl. Onion rings may be added just before serving.

Lemon carrots

Serves 8
Per serving: 38 KCal, 5.4 g carbohydrate, 0.8 g protein, 1.5 g fat,
0 mg cholesterol, 2.7 g fibre, 169 mg sodium

170 g/6 oz carrots, sliced about   *15 ml/1 tbsp lemon juice*
* 0.5 cm/¼ in thick*   *15 g/1 tbsp fresh chopped chives*
15 g/½ oz margarine

Combine the first 3 ingredients in a saucepan, add 75 ml/3 fl oz
water and cover. Cook over a medium heat until just tender, about
10–15 minutes. Add the chopped chives and serve immediately.

An alternative   You may substitute fresh chopped parsley for
the chives.

Carrot purée

Serves 6
Per serving: 53 KCal, 9.1 g carbohydrate, 2.9 g protein, 0.6 g fat, 0 mg cholesterol, 5.4 g fibre, 108 mg sodium

170 g/6 oz carrots, sliced
40 g/1½ oz oat bran cereal
50 ml/2 fl oz skimmed milk
artificial sweetener to taste
2.5 ml/½ tsp salt (optional)

2.5 ml/½ tsp cinnamon
1.25 ml/¼ tsp nutmeg
15–30 g/1–2 tbsp chopped nuts
(optional)

Heat oven to 190°C/375°F/gas 5.
  In a large saucepan, bring 225 ml/8 fl oz water to the boil. Add the carrots and cover. Simmer until tender, about 10–12 minutes. Transfer the carrots with water to a food processor or blender goblet in batches. Blend until smooth. Add all the remaining ingredients except the nuts; blend again until smooth. At this point, the purée may be put into a covered ovenproof dish and stored in the refrigerator until ready to bake. Bake for about 30 minutes or until heated through. Sprinkle with nuts, if using. Serve immediately.

Courgette casserole

Serves 8
Per serving: 103 KCal, 7.5 carbohydrate, 6.2 g protein, 5.4 g fat, 7 mg cholesterol, 4.5 g fibre, 143 mg sodium

700 g/1½ lb courgette, grated
15 ml/1 tbsp vegetable oil
115 g/4 oz onion, chopped
75 g/3 oz oat bran
50 g/2 oz low-fat cheese, grated

2.5 ml/½ tsp dried basil or oregano
2.5 ml/½ tsp salt (optional)
1.25 ml/¼ tsp pepper
75 g/3 oz tinned tomatoes
5 ml/1 tsp tomato purée

Heat oven to 190°C/375°F /gas 5.
  Lightly oil a 20 cm/8 in square ovenproof dish. Squeeze the courgette between paper towels to remove the excess moisture. Heat the oil in a small frying pan. Sauté the onion until tender, about 3–4 minutes. Transfer to a large bowl. Add the courgette and all the remaining ingredients, except the tomatoes and purée. Mix well. Pour into the prepared dish. Mix the tomatoes with the purée and spread evenly over the top. Bake for 30 minutes.

Courgette casserole (*top*), Carrot purée (*bottom*)

Baked marrow

Serves 6
Per serving: 85 KCal, 10.8 g carbohydrate, 7.5 g protein, 1.3 g fat,
1 mg cholesterol, 6.2 g fibre, 135 mg sodium

900 g/2 lb marrow
50 g/2 oz onion, chopped
1 stick celery, diced
170 g/6 oz cottage cheese, sieved

50 g/2 oz rolled oats
2.5 ml/½ tsp mixed dried herbs
225 g/8 oz carrots, grated

Heat oven to 180°C /350°F /gas 4.
Cook together the marrow, onion, celery and seasoning salt in
115 ml/4 fl oz water, until just tender. Drain. Add the carrots, cottage cheese, oats and mixed dried herbs. Pour into a lightly greased ovenproof dish. Bake for about 20 minutes.

Stuffed peppers See photograph, page 72

Serves 4
Per serving: 109 KCal, 20.6 g carbohydrate, 4.6 g protein, 0.9 g fat,
0 mg cholesterol, 4.7 g fibre, 366 g sodium

100 g/3 oz cooked brown lentils (see page 76)
115 g/4 oz brown rice, cooked (see page 82)
15 ml/1 tbsp chopped onion
pinch sweet basil (optional)
5 ml/1 tsp parsley, chopped

2.5 ml/½ tsp garlic salt
freshly ground black pepper
approximately 60 ml/2 fl oz light stock
75 ml/3 fl oz tomato juice
4 medium peppers, halved and seeded

Heat oven to 170°C/325°F /gas 3.
Mix together the lentils, rice and onion. Add basil, if using, parsley, garlic salt and pepper. Add the stock and tomato juice and mix to a soft consistency. Stuff the peppers with the lentil and rice mixture. Place in a lightly greased ovenproof dish, cover with foil and bake for 45 minutes.

Pimiento green beans See photograph, page 72

Serves 8
Per serving: 75KCal, 11.5 g carbohydrate, 2.7 g protein, 2.0 g fat,
0 mg cholesterol, 3.4 g fibre, 143 mg sodium

450 g/1 lb green beans, fresh or frozen
½ green pepper, chopped
2.5 ml/½ tsp salt (optional)

250 g/9 oz cooked rice (see page 82)
25 g/1 oz toasted almonds
40 g/1½ oz pimiento, chopped

Cook the green beans and green pepper in lightly salted boiling water until just tender, or according to packet instructions. Drain and stir in the rice. Pour into a serving bowl and top with toasted almonds and pimiento.

Hash brown potatoes

Serves 2
Per serving: 102 KCal, 22.2 g carbohydrate, 2.8 g protein, 0.2 g fat, 0 mg cholesterol, 3.7 g fibre, 10 mg sodium

1 large potato   *30 ml/2 tbsp onion, diced*
25 ml/½ tsp cooking oil   *seasoning*

Cut the potato into cubes, cook in boiling water until tender and drain. Heat the oil in a non-stick frying pan and sauté the onion. Add salt and pepper to the drained potato cubes, then brown the cubes with the onion over medium heat.

Ratatouille   See photograph, page 72

Serves 8
Per serving: 93 KCal, 11.6 g carbohydrate, 3.2 g protein, 3.8 g fat, 0 mg cholesterol, 4.8 g fibre, 234 mg sodium

30 ml/2 tbsp cooking oil   *2 green peppers, chopped*
1 medium aubergine, cut into   *1 cucumber, peeled and sliced*
  2.5 cm/1 in pieces   *0.5 cm/¼ in thick*
1 medium courgette, sliced   *2 cloves garlic, crushed*
  0.5 cm/¼ in thick   *170 ml/6 fl oz tomato purée*
225 g/8 oz onions, sliced   *2.5 ml/½ tsp dried oregano*
4 medium tomatoes, quartered   *dash of tabasco sauce*

Heat the oil in a large saucepan. Add half the vegetables and sauté for 1–2 minutes. Add the remaining vegetables and sauté for a further minute. Simmer for 15 minutes, stirring occasionally. Add the tomato purée, oregano and tabasco. Simmer for 40–45 minutes, stirring occasionally, until the vegetables are soft. Serve accompanied by wholemeal bread, or over rice.

OVERLEAF: Ratatouille (*top right*), Stuffed peppers (*top left*, see page 70), Pimiento green beans (*bottom*, see page 70)

Stuffed tomatoes

Serves 6
Per serving: 88 KCal, 13.3 g carbohydrate, 4.9 g protein, 1.7 g fat, 4 mg cholesterol, 5.3 g fibre, 281 mg sodium

6 large tomatoes
2.5 ml/½ tsp onion salt
75 g/3 oz sweetcorn kernels
75 g/3 oz marrow or *courgette, finely chopped*

15 ml/1 tbsp green pepper, chopped
25 g/1 oz rolled oats
25 g/1 oz low-fat cheese, grated

Heat oven to 180°C/350°F/gas 4.
   Cut a thin slice from the stem end of each tomato, and remove the pulp and core, leaving the sides intact. Place the pulp, onion salt, sweetcorn, marrow and pepper in a saucepan and cook for 5–8 minutes until just tender. Add the oats and cheese and mix well. Stuff the tomatoes and place in a flat ovenproof dish. Cover and bake for 20–25 minutes.

Vegetable medley

Serves 6
Per serving: 64 KCal, 3.8 g carbohydrate, 1.5 g protein, 4.7 g fat, 0 mg cholesterol, 1.9 g fibre, 110 mg sodium

30 ml/2 tbsp vegetable oil
50 g/2 oz carrots, cut into long strips
170 g/6 oz mangetout peas
25 g/1 oz mushrooms, halved
50 g/2 oz cherry tomatoes

50 g/2 oz broccoli, chopped
50 g/2 oz cauliflower florets
1 small onion, chopped
15 ml/1 tbsp cooking sherry
15 ml/1 tbsp soy sauce (optional)

Heat 7.5 ml/1½ tsp of oil in a large non-stick frying pan. Add the carrots and cook, stirring frequently until just tender, about 3 minutes. Stir in the mangetout and cook for a further 2 minutes. Place in a warmed serving dish. Add 7.5 ml/1½ tsp of oil to the pan and stir in the mushrooms. Cook, stirring, until lightly browned. Stir in the tomatoes and cook for 1 minute. Add to the mangetout and carrots. Stir in the remaining 15 ml/1 tbsp vegetable oil and remaining vegetables. Cook for about 2 minutes, stirring constantly. Add 115 ml/4 fl oz water and the sherry and cook until just tender, about 7–8 minutes. Mix all the vegetables together and add the soy sauce. Serve hot or cold.

Stir-fried vegetables

Serves 4
Per serving: 106 KCal, 11.8 g carbohydrate, 3.6 g protein, 4.9 g fat, 0 mg cholesterol, 4.6 g fibre, 182 mg sodium

225 g/8 oz fresh broccoli
2 sticks celery
1 medium size fresh tomato
115 g/4 oz fresh mushrooms
150 g/5 oz water chestnuts, tinned
75 g/3 oz onion

20 ml/4 tsp corn oil
artificial sweetener, to taste
15 ml/1 tbsp soy sauce
5 ml/1 tsp cornflour
1.25 ml/¼ tsp pepper

Wash the vegetables. Cut the broccoli into stems and florets and then dice florets into bite-size pieces. Quarter the broccoli and celery stems lengthwise, then slant cut into small pieces. Slice tomato, mushrooms and drained water chestnuts. Dice onion. Heat oil in a frying pan over medium-high heat. Add the vegetables and stir them constantly for about 2 minutes. Add the artificial sweetener and 60 ml/2 fl oz water, cover and cook 1 minute. Mix the soy sauce and cornflour with 2.5 ml/½ tsp water. Add this to the vegetables and cook about 30 seconds, stirring constantly until sauce is thick and clear.

BEANS AND PULSES

Beans and pulses are among the best food bargains you can find and are high in protein and fibre. They are also very versatile and enhance salads and casseroles. As we explained in the introduction, for two reasons beans are one of the best health-promoting foods: they stabilize your blood sugar and lower your blood cholesterol. After a serving of beans your blood sugar does not shoot up nearly as high as after other carbohydrate foods such as white bread or potatoes, and so you are less susceptible to later resulting low blood sugars. Beans and oats are rich in the gummy or water-soluble type of fibre that lowers the blood cholesterol. Two servings of beans daily as a part of the HCF diet can lower your cholesterol by 20 per cent, or 50 mg per 100 ml.

Fortunately tinned beans deliver the same benefits as home-cooked beans. Because of their convenience, my wife and I frequently use tinned beans, and they can be used in most of the recipes included. Bean burritos are among my favourites, and our family has them at least once a week. They may be frozen and reheated quickly for a snack or a light meal.

If you want to use dried beans (more economical than tinned), here's the way to cook them: soak overnight in cold water or alternatively place in cold water, bring to the boil, boil for 2–3 minutes then cover and leave to soak for one hour. The beans will have doubled in weight. To cook, cover with fresh, unsalted water and boil rapidly for the first 10 minutes. Then cover and simmer gently. Total cooking times vary for the different beans. The following need 30 minutes, or 10 minutes in a pressure cooker: aduki and mung beans, peas; 30 minutes–1 hour (15–20 minutes in a pressure cooker): black–eyed beans and Continental lentils (brown or green); 1–2 hours (½–1 hour in a pressure cooker): broad and butter beans, chick peas, haricot, red speckled Mexican, and red kidney beans; 3–4 hours (1–1½ hours in a pressure cooker): soya beans. Add salt (in moderation) and other flavouring only after this cooking, to prevent the beans becoming tough.

Red or Egyptian lentils and split peas do not need soaking and take only about 30 minutes to cook.

The salt-content of bean dishes varies. Beans cooked at home without salt are low in sodium. Some tinned beans have 700 – 1000 mg of sodium per 225 g/8 oz. Draining beans and rinsing them with clear water eliminates about half the salt content. To limit your salt intake for certain recipes we recommend using rinsed tinned beans or beans cooked at home.

Bean burritos

Serves 8
Per serving: 238 KCal, 39.7 g carbohydrate, 12.9 g protein, 3.1 g fat, 5 mg cholesterol, 13.6 g fibre, 206 mg sodium

900 g/2 lb refried beans (see page 80)   *75 g/3 oz chopped onions*
8 wheat tortillas, 23 cm/9 in diameter   *20 ml/4 tsp taco sauce*
                                              50 g/2 oz grated cheddar cheese

Place tortillas on a baking sheet and heat in a low oven for a few minutes to make them pliable. Put 115 g/4 oz refried beans on the centre of each flattened tortilla. Spread the onions over and push into the beans. Sprinkle 2.5 ml/½ tsp taco sauce over each tortilla and top with the cheese. Fold sides to middle, to make oblong burritos and place in an ovenproof dish. Heat through in a low oven for 15–20 minutes. Add more taco sauce on top according to taste.

Bean burritos

Hearty bean barley dish

Serves 2
Per serving: 239 KCal, 46.3 g carbohydrate, 11.3 g protein, 1 g fat,
0 mg cholesterol, 10.7 g fibre, 453 mg sodium

115 ml/4 fl oz tomato juice
50 g/2 oz uncooked barley
50 g/2 oz uncooked red lentils
2 sticks celery, chopped
½ medium onion, sliced

50 g/2 oz raw potatoes, diced
50 g/2 oz carrot, diced
15 ml/1 tbsp mixed dried herbs
2.5 ml/½ tsp salt

Simmer the tomato juice, 50 ml/2 fl oz water, the barley and lentils for 15 minutes. Add the vegetables and herbs and seasoning,
and continue to simmer for another 30 minutes.

Kidney beans and rice

Serves 2
Per serving: 210 KCal, 39 g carbohydrate, 10.7 g protein, 1.2 g fat,
0 mg cholesterol, 13.4 g fibre, 8 mg sodium

1 bay leaf
115 g/4 oz cooked kidney beans (see
  page 76)
115 g/4 oz raw onion, diced
115 g/4 oz green pepper, diced

2.5 ml/½ tsp garlic salt
seasoning
115 g/4 oz brown rice, cooked (see
  page 82)

Combine the first 5 ingredients in a saucepan. Season to taste.
Heat until the onions and green pepper are cooked. Remove the
bay leaf and serve over the brown rice.

Curried succotash

Serves 2
Per serving: 155 KCal, 20.8 carbohydrate, 7.7 g protein, 4.6 g fat,
0 mg cholesterol, 11.4 g fibre, 261 mg sodium

50 g/2 oz fresh celery, diced – do not
  strip off fibres
10 ml/2 tsp corn oil margarine
115 g/4 oz tinned or cooked butter
  beans, drained

115 g/4 oz sweetcorn kernels, drained
30 ml/2 tbsp chopped pimiento
5 ml/1 tsp curry powder, or to taste
pinch of salt (optional)

In a large frying pan, sauté the celery in margarine until tender.
Add the beans and sweetcorn, cover and cook for 8–10 minutes

over medium heat. Add the pimiento, mix in the curry powder and salt, and continue cooking for a few minutes to blend the curry flavour.

Hearty bean bake

Serves 4

Per serving: 130 KCal, 22.9 g carbohydrate, 7.4 g protein, 1 g fat, 0 mg cholesterol, 9.3 g fibre, 415 mg sodium

50 g/2 oz onion, finely chopped
1 clove garlic, crushed
450 g/1 lb tin baked beans
170 g/6 oz cooked kidney beans

75 g/3 oz cooked butter beans (see page 76)
50 g/2 oz tomato ketchup
5 ml/1 tsp prepared mustard
pepper

Heat oven to 190°C/375°F/gas 5.

Combine all the ingredients in an ovenproof dish. Bake for 45 minutes. Stir before serving.

Refried beans

Serves 8

Per serving: 127 KCal, 16.8 g carbohydrate, 10.1 g protein, 2.2 g fat, 3 mg cholesterol, 12.6 g fibre, 275 mg sodium

2 slices lean bacon
225 g/8 oz chopped onions

2 × 450 g/1 lb tins Mexican or red kidney beans
10 ml/2 tsp garlic salt

In a large frying pan fry the bacon until crisp. Remove from the pan; cook the onions in the bacon fat until tender. Crumble the bacon and add to the frying pan with the beans and garlic salt. Mash with a potato masher. Cook over low heat for 10 minutes stirring frequently, until dry. Serve as a side dish or use for bean burritos (see page 76).

Bavarian beans

Serves 4

Per serving: 242 KCal, 22.5 g carbohydrate, 15.5 g protein, 10 g fat, 21 mg cholesterol, 8.4 g fibre, 597 mg sodium

140 g/5 oz cabbage, shredded
50 g/2 oz onion, chopped
25 g/1 oz margarine
450 g/1 lb tin baked beans, rinsed and drained

170 g/6 oz cooked lean pork, diced
15 ml/1 tbsp prepared mustard
pinch crushed thyme leaves
5 ml/1 tsp vinegar

In a frying pan, cook the cabbage and onion in the margarine until tender. Add the remaining ingredients. Heat, stirring occasionally; add a little water if necessary to prevent sticking.

Calico beans

Serves 4
Per serving: 293 KCal, 36.6 g carbohydrate, 20.5 g protein, 7.2 g fat, 42 mg cholesterol, 13.2 g fibre, 529 mg sodium

225 g/8 oz lean minced beef   *280 g/10 oz sweetcorn kernels*
1.25 ml/¼ tsp ground cumin
1.25 ml/¼ tsp pepper   Garnish:
115 g/4 oz onion, chopped   *shredded lettuce*
450 g/1 lb tin baked beans, rinsed *chopped tomato*
  and drained

Season minced beef with half the cumin and pepper. Shape into 12 meat balls. In a frying pan, brown the meat balls with the onion until tender. Pour off any fat. Add the beans, sweetcorn and remaining cumin. Heat, stirring occasionally; add a little water if necessary to prevent sticking. Garnish with lettuce and tomato.

Barbecue butter beans

Serves 8
Per serving: 82 KCal, 13.9 g carbohydrate, 5.8 g protein, 0.4 g fat, 0 mg cholesterol, 6.3 g fibre, 198 mg sodium

225 g/8 oz dried butter beans   *1.25 ml/¼ tsp dry mustard*
1 ham bone   *2.5 ml/½ tsp malt vinegar*
½ medium onion, sliced   *5 ml/1 tsp artificial sweetener*
1.25 ml/¼ tsp salt   *45 ml/3 tbsp chilli sauce*

Place the beans in a large saucepan with the ham bone. Add 900 ml/1½ pints water. Bring to the boil and boil for 2 minutes; remove from heat, cover tightly and let stand 1 hour.
  Heat oven to 150°C/300°F/gas 2.
  Drain beans, reserving 225 ml/8 fl oz liquid. Combine beans and reserved liquid with remaining ingredients. Bake in an ovenproof dish for 2¼ hours, uncovering for the last 30 minutes. Add more liquid if necessary.

RICE DISHES

Like the other grains, rice is an excellent source of vitamins and other nutrients, and is not a fattening food eaten instead of ,rather than as well as, high-protein foods. Brown rice contains a lot more fibre, so it is usually a better choice than white rice for the HCF diet. We have included recipes for both types so you can choose which you prefer, according to nutritional value and taste.

For most savoury dishes, choose long grain rice, whether brown or white. This keeps its shape and retains a bite when cooked. For creamy puddings and smoother risottos use round-grain, Carolina or risotto rice.

Cooking long-grain rice

On average, allow 40 – 50 g/1½–2 oz uncooked rice per person. Rinse in cold water to get rid of extra starch, place in a saucepan and cover with 1½ times the quantity of lightly salted boiling water. Bring back to the boil, stir once, cover tightly and reduce heat. Simmer gently without stirring until the rice is cooked and all the liquid absorbed (about 15–20 minutes for white rice, 25–30 minutes for brown). Fluff with a fork.

Remember, cooked rice is about double its equivalent uncooked. If cooked rice is required in the recipes, this is always stated. Otherwise use uncooked rice as directed.

Rice: nutrient and fibre content

Values as grams per 100 grams (approximately 3½ oz) cooked rice

	KCal	Carbohydrate	Protein	Fat	Cholesterol	Fibre	Sodium
White rice	111	24.5	2.1	0.2	0	0.8	10 mg
Brown rice	111	23.1	2.5	0.6	0	2.4	10 mg

Spanish rice

Serves 6
Per serving: 157 KCal, 28 g carbohydrate, 6.1 g protein, 2.3 g fat, 6 mg cholesterol, 4.4 g fibre, 237 mg sodium ➔

Harvest rice (*top*, see page 84), Spanish rice (*bottom*)

450 ml/16 fl oz tomato juice
50 g/2 oz onion, finely chopped
225 g/8 oz brown rice
2 sticks celery, finely diced
1 green pepper, diced

280 g/10 oz tomatoes, chopped
2.5 ml/½ tsp oregano
2.5 ml/½ tsp basil
pinch of pepper
50 g/2 oz low-fat cheese, grated

Bring the tomato juice, onion and rice to the boil, cover and simmer for 25 minutes. Add all the remaining ingredients except the cheese. Continue cooking for about 20 minutes. Pour into a warmed serving dish and top with the cheese.

Harvest rice

See photograph, page 83

Serves 6
Per serving: 248 KCal, 46.7 g carbohydrate, 3.4 g protein, 5.3 g fat, 0 mg cholesterol, 4.8 g fibre, 173 mg sodium

75 g/3 oz carrots, thinly sliced
25 g/1 oz margarine
170 ml/6 oz apple juice
30 ml/2 tbsp lemon juice
25 g/1 oz brown sugar
225 g/8 oz long-grain rice
2.5 ml/½ tsp ground cinnamon

75 g/3 oz raisins
50 g/2 oz spring onions, sliced
335 g/12 oz unpeeled apples, cored and
  sliced
15 ml/1 tbsp toasted sesame seeds
  (optional)

Cook the carrots gently in the margarine until just tender, about 5 minutes. Add the apple and lemon juice together with 280 ml/10 fl oz water, and the brown sugar. Bring to the boil. Stir in the rice, cinnamon and raisins. Reduce heat, cover and simmer until the rice is tender and the liquid absorbed, about 15 minutes. Gently stir in the spring onions and apples; heat through. Turn into a serving dish. Top with sesame seeds if using.

Rice jardin

Serves 3
Per serving: 166 KCal, 25.5 g carbohydrate, 4 g protein, 5.3 g fat, 0 mg cholesterol, 6.2 g fibre, 228 mg sodium

50 g/2 oz chopped onion
115 g/4 oz courgette, thinly sliced
15 ml/1 tbsp corn oil
150 g/5 oz sweetcorn kernels
150 g/5 oz tinned tomatoes, drained

115 g/4 oz cooked brown rice (see
  page 82)
2.5 ml/½ tsp salt
1.5 ml/¼ tsp pepper
pinch of dried oregano
2.5 ml/½ tsp chilli powder

Sauté the onion and courgette in the oil until tender. Add remaining ingredients. Cover and simmer for 15 minutes.

Baked mushroom rice

Serves 6

Per serving: 121 KCal, 19.5 g carbohydrate, 4.4 g protein, 2.8 g fat, 0 mg cholesterol, 2.3 g fibre, 200 mg sodium

225 g/8 oz long-grain rice
50 g/2 oz spring onions, sliced
15 g/½ oz margarine
65 g/2½ oz tinned sliced mushrooms with liquid

50 g/2 oz chopped pimientos
335 ml/12 fl oz chicken stock
50 ml/2 fl oz dry cooking sherry
2.5 ml/½ tsp pepper

Heat oven to 190°C/375°F/gas 5.

Sprinkle rice in a lightly greased ovenproof dish. Fry the onions in the margarine until soft. Add remaining ingredients. Bring to the boil. Pour over the rice; stir. Cover with a tight-fitting lid or foil. Bake for 25–30 minutes or until rice is tender and liquid has been absorbed. Fluff lightly with a fork.

Fruited rice

Serves 6

Per serving: 220 KCal, 38.1 g carbohydrate, 3.5 g protein, 5.9 g fat, 0 mg cholesterol, 5.2 g fibre, 119 mg sodium

75 g/3 oz carrots, sliced
30 ml/2 tbsp vegetable oil
115 g/4 oz spring onions, sliced
335 g/12 oz unpeeled apples, sliced and cored

500 g/1 lb 2 oz cooked brown rice (see page 82)
75 g/3 oz seedless raisins
15 ml/1 tbsp toasted sesame seeds (optional)

Cook the carrots in the oil for about 10 minutes. Add the onions and apples. Cook for a further 10 minutes. Stir in the rice and raisins. Cook, stirring, until the rice is heated through. Add sesame seeds, if using, and toss lightly.

Cumin rice

Serves 6

Per serving: 125 KCal, 22.8 g carbohydrate, 2.5 g protein, 2.6 g fat, 0 mg cholesterol, 2.6 g fibre, 405 mg sodium

50 g/2 oz onion, chopped
50 g/2 oz green pepper, chopped
225 g/8 oz long-grain rice
15 ml/1 tbsp vegetable oil

225 ml/8 fl oz beef stock or consommé
15 ml/1 tbsp Worcestershire sauce
5 ml/1 tsp cumin seed

Heat oven to 180°C/350°F/gas 4.

Over a low heat fry the onion, pepper and rice in vegetable oil until the rice is golden brown. Stir constantly to prevent overbrowning. Turn into a shallow ovenproof casserole. Add remaining ingredients together with 225 ml/8 fl oz water; stir well. Cover tightly with a lid or foil and bake for 30 minutes or until rice is tender and liquid absorbed. Fluff lightly with a fork.

FISH, MEAT AND POULTRY AND MAIN DISH CASSEROLES

We have found eating smaller quantities of meat has been an easy and enjoyable changeover. We have chicken twice a week, beef once a week and fish when we eat out. Usually we stir-fry chicken or beef with vegetables, or include it in a casserole. We did not find it difficult giving up steak, roast beef, ham or pork chops and now eat them only on special occasions in restaurants. Over the last few years we have started making meatless pasta dishes, chilli and stuffed green peppers. In the recipes I have given you suggestions on how to make delicious main dishes without using excessive amounts of red meat or poultry.

FISH

Sole Florentine

Serves 8
Per serving: 162 KCal, 9.6 g carbohydrate, 14.7 g protein, 7.2 g fat, 34 mg cholesterol, 6.8 g fibre, 148 mg sodium

1 × 225 g/8 oz packet frozen chopped spinach
40 g/1½ oz margarine
50 g/2 oz mushrooms, sliced
50 g/2 oz spring onion, chopped
140 g/5 oz medium oatmeal

1 egg white (optional)
5 ml/1 tsp salt (optional)
50 ml/2 fl oz lemon juice
8 sole or haddock fillets
paprika pepper

Sole Florentine

Heat oven to 190°C/375°F/gas 5.
Thaw spinach, reserving liquid. In a medium frying pan, melt the margarine. Sauté the mushrooms and onion over a medium heat for 3–4 minutes. Add oats, egg white if using, salt if using, 30 ml/2 tbsp lemon juice, spinach and reserved liquid; mix well. Spread the oat mixture evenly over the fillets. Roll up; place seam side down in a shallow non-stick baking dish. Sprinkle with remaining lemon juice; dust with paprika pepper. Cover with foil and cook for 25 minutes or until the fish flakes easily with a fork.

Lemon baked fish

Serves 4
Per serving: 165 KCal, 3.9 g carbohydrate, 26.0 g protein, 5.0 g fat, 102 mg cholesterol, 0 g fibre, 237 mg sodium

700 g/1½ lb plaice, haddock or other   20 ml/4 tsp lemon juice
*   white fish fillet, fresh or frozen   seasoning*
15 g/½ oz margarine, melted   1.25 ml/¼ tsp dried basil
5 ml/1 tsp grated lemon rind

Heat oven to 180°C/350°F/gas 4.
Thaw fish, if using frozen ,and place in an ovenproof dish. Blend together the remaining ingredients and pour over the fish. Cover with foil and cook for 20–25 minutes or until fish flakes easily when tested with a fork.

Honey-curried fish

Serves 3
Per serving: 154 KCal, 1.6 g carbohydrate, 27.6 g protein, 4.1 g fat, 83 mg cholesterol, 0 g fibre, 185 mg sodium

450 g/1 lb fish fillets   1.25 ml/¼ tsp curry powder, or
15 ml/1 tbsp Dijon mustard   according to taste
15 ml/3 tsp honey
10 ml/2 tsp lemon juice   Garnish:
*   chopped parsley*
*   paprika pepper*

Heat oven to 180°C/350°F/gas 4.
Place the fish in a small ovenproof casserole. Mix together the remaining ingredients and pour over the fish. Cook for 25 minutes, then place under a hot grill for 2 minutes. Garnish with chopped parsley and paprika.

Summer-light tuna salad

Serves 4
Per serving: 179 KCal, 15 g carbohydrate, 19.3 g protein, 4.6 g fat,
30 mg cholesterol, 2.6 g fibre, 212 mg sodium

1 stick celery, sliced
170 ml/6 fl oz plain low-fat yoghurt
1 × 200 g/7 oz tin tuna in brine, drained
30 ml/2 tbsp mixed pickle
50 ml/2 oz toasted oats (see below)
45 ml/3 tbsp chopped onion or *spring onion*
lettuce leaves or *tomatoes, sliced*

Mix together the first 6 ingredients. Chill. Serve on lettuce or sliced tomato.

Toasted oats Heat oven to 180°C/350°F/gas 4. Spread 170 g/6 oz rolled oats on an ungreased baking sheet and bake 15–20 minutes or until light golden brown. Cool and store in a tightly covered container in the refrigerator.
  Toasted oats are a good topping for salads and puddings, and a substitute for breadcrumbs, wheat bran or wheat germ.

Cantonese prawns with rice

Serves 6   See photograph, page 90
Per serving: 233 KCal, 33.5 g carbohydrate, 17.0 g protein, 3.4 g fat, 112 mg cholesterol, 4.3 g fibre, 494 mg sodium

170 g/6 oz rice
15 ml/1 tbsp vegetable oil
335 g/12 oz peeled raw prawns, halved lengthwise
2 sticks celery, sliced diagonally
140 g/5 oz onions, chopped
225 g/8 oz leaf spinach, coarsely shredded
280 g/10 oz frozen mixed vegetables

Sauce variation:
1.25 ml/¼ tsp pepper
225 ml/½ pint chicken stock
30 ml/2 tbsp cornflour

Cook rice (see page 82), cover and keep warm.
  Heat the oil in a large frying pan or wok, add prawns and cook until they just turn pink. Stir in the celery and onions and cook for about 2 minutes. Add spinach and mixed vegetables. Cover and cook for a further 2 minutes. Serve with the rice.

Variation Blend together the sauce ingredients and stir into the prawn and vegetable mixture. Cook until the sauce has thickened, about 2 minutes.

OVERLEAF: Cantonese prawns with rice (*bottom and top right*), Oriental kebabs (*left*, see page 92)

MEAT

Oriental kebabs

See photograph, page 90

Serves 6
Per serving: 274 KCal, 4.6 g carbohydrate, 30 g protein, 15.1 g fat,
100 mg cholesterol, 0.5 g fibre, 76 (360) mg sodium*

700 g/1½ lb pork tenderloin
115 ml/4 fl oz unsweetened
  pineapple juice
115 ml/4 fl oz soy sauce
15 ml/1 tbsp celery seed
2.5 ml/½ tsp ground ginger

1 clove garlic, crushed
pinch of pepper
½ red pepper
½ green pepper
5 ml/1 tsp cornflour

Cut the tenderloin into 2.5 cm/1 in pieces. Mix together the
pineapple juice, soy sauce, celery seed, ginger, garlic and pepper.
Pour over the tenderloin, cover and chill overnight or for 2 hours
at room temperature.

Remove meat from marinade and thread on 6 skewers, alternat-
ing with red and green peppers cut into 2.5 cm/1 in squares. Mix
together the reserved marinade with 30 ml/2 tbsp water and the
cornflour. Brush the kebabs with the marinade mixture. Cook
under a hot grill for 12–15 minutes. Turn and brush with marinade
during cooking.

Beef shish kebabs

Serves 8
Per serving: 235 KCal, 5.1 g carbohydrate, 29.2 g protein, 10.9 g
fat, 55 mg cholesterol, 2.5 g fibre, 117 (387) mg sodium*

700 g/1½ lb lean rump steak
115 ml/4 fl oz soy sauce
50 ml/2 fl oz Worcestershire sauce
30 ml/2 tbsp vegetable oil
50 ml/2 fl oz red wine

1 clove garlic, crushed
5 ml/1 tsp dry mustard
3 green peppers, cut in strips
12 large mushrooms
12 cherry tomatoes

Cut steak into 2.5 cm/1 in cubes. Mix together the soy sauce,
Worcestershire sauce, oil, wine, garlic and mustard. Pour over the
meat. Cover and chill overnight or at room temperature for 2–3
hours, turning the meat occasionally.

Thread the meat, peppers, mushrooms and tomatoes alter-
nately on skewers. Cook under a hot grill, turning frequently, for
12–15 minutes.

---

*First value is without soy sauce, value in parentheses includes reduced-
salt soy sauce (available from health food shops).

Beef ginger

Serves 6
Per serving: 436 KCal, 34.2 g carbohydrate, 41.3 g protein, 14.9 g
fat, 74 mg cholesterol, 4.6 g fibre, 145 (325) mg sodium*

700 g/1½ lb rump steak
30 ml/2 tbsp vegetable oil
1 onion, sliced and separated into
  rings
2 sticks celery, diagonally sliced
75 g/3 oz carrots, thinly sliced
1 green pepper, cut into strips

50 g/2 oz mushrooms, sliced
15 ml/1 tbsp cornflour
50 ml/2 fl oz soy sauce
225 g/8 oz tomato ketchup
1.25 ml/¼ tsp ground ginger
500 g/1 lb 2 oz cooked rice (see
  page 82)

Prepare all the ingredients ready for cooking. Trim steak of any
excess fat and cut in thin slices about 5 cm/2 in long. Heat oil in a
large frying pan or wok. Brown the steak, push aside and add
onion, celery and carrots. Stir-fry until tender, about 3–4 minutes.
Push vegetables to the side and add green pepper and mushrooms.
Stir-fry for 1 minute. Mix together the cornflour, soy sauce,
tomato ketchup and ginger. Add to the frying pan. Stir until sauce
thickens. Serve with the hot rice.

Pepper steak   See photograph, page 94

Serves 6
Per serving: 383 KCal, 27.4 g carbohydrate, 39.8 g protein, 12.7 g
fat, 74 mg cholesterol, 3.6 g fibre, 260 (440) mg sodium*

2.5 ml/½ tsp paprika
15 ml/1 tbsp cornflour
60 ml/4 tbsp soy sauce
225 g/8 oz lean rump steak, cut into
  0.5 cm/¼ in strips
15 ml/1 tbsp vegetable oil

3 medium green peppers, cut into
  0.5 cm/¼ in strips
approximately 225 ml/8 fl oz beef
  stock
500 g/1 lb 2 oz cooked brown or white
  rice (see page 82)

Mix together the paprika, cornflour and half the soy sauce and
pour over the meat. Marinate the meat for 10 minutes.
   Heat the oil in a wok or large non-stick frying pan and add the
green peppers. Stir constantly until tender, about 4–5 minutes.
Remove to a dish. Stir-fry about one half of the meat for 2–4
minutes. Add to peppers, cook the remaining meat, then return
the meat and peppers to the frying pan. Add the stock and remaining soy sauce and cook about 5 minutes, until tender. Serve over
the hot rice.

*See note, page 92.

Beef stroganoff

Serves 6
Per serving: 317 KCal, 4.7 g carbohydrate, 42 g protein, 14.5 g fat,
75 mg cholesterol, 1.5 g fibre, 341 mg sodium

700 g/1½ lb rump steak, partially	*115 g/4 oz mushrooms, sliced*
frozen	*30 ml/2 tbsp wholemeal flour*
30 ml/2 tbsp vegetable oil	*225 ml/8 fl oz beef stock*
2 large onions, chopped	*170 g/6 oz cottage cheese, sieved*

Cut partially frozen steak across the grain into strips about
0.5 × 5 cm/¼ × 2 in. Heat 15 ml/1 tbsp of the oil in a large frying
pan. Add the onions and mushrooms and cook gently until soft.
Remove the vegetables with a slotted spoon and set aside. Add the
remaining tablespoon of oil and quickly brown the steak strips, a
few at a time. Remove and add to the vegetables. Stir in the flour,
add the stock and bring to the boil, stirring constantly until
slightly thickened. Add the vegetable and meat mixture to the
sauce and bring to the boil. Add the sieved cottage cheese and
serve immediately with hot rice or noodles.

Baked beef and potatoes

Serves 6
Per serving: 184 KCal, 16.1 g carbohydrate, 12.0 g protein, 8.0 g
fat, 29 mg cholesterol, 2.8 g fibre, 271 mg sodium

115 g/4 oz carrots, sliced	*40 g/1½ oz wholemeal flour*
225 g/8 oz potatoes, sliced	*2.5 ml/½ tsp salt*
225 g/8 oz lean minced beef	*pinch of pepper*
1 medium onion, chopped	*335 ml/12 fl oz skimmed milk*
½ green pepper, chopped	*5 ml/1 tsp dry mustard*
25 g/1 oz margarine	

Heat oven to 180°C/350°F/gas 4.
Cook the carrots and potatoes in 170 ml/6 fl oz water until just
tender. Drain well. Brown the beef, onion and green pepper; drain
off any excess fat. Melt the margarine, stir in the flour and cook
over a low heat for 1–2 minutes, then pour on the warmed milk,
stirring constantly. Season and add the mustard.
In an ovenproof dish layer the potatoes and carrots with the
meat mixture. Repeat layers and finish with the sauce. Bake
uncovered for 25–30 minutes.

Pepper steak (*top*, see page 93), Beef stroganoff (*bottom*)

Surprise meat balls

Serves 6
Per serving: 457 KCal, 42 g carbohydrate, 37.5 g protein, 15.4 g fat,
88 mg cholesterol, 7.5 g fibre, 369 mg sodium

700 g/1½ lb lean minced beef
170 g/6 oz cottage cheese
25 g/1 oz mozzarella cheese, grated
75 g/3 oz onions, finely chopped
25 g/1 oz egg replacer or 1 egg white,
* lightly beaten*
280 g/10 oz frozen spinach, thawed
* and drained*
50 g/2 oz rolled oats

1.25 ml/¼ tsp pepper
1.25 ml/¼ tsp garlic powder
225 ml/8 fl oz beef stock
115 ml/4 fl oz tomato purée mixed
* with 60 ml/4 tbsp water*
50 ml/2 fl oz cooking sherry
30 ml/2 tbsp cornflour
500 g/1 lb 2 oz cooked rice

Heat oven to 230°C/450°F/gas 8.

Mix together the meat, cheeses, onion, egg replacer or egg white, spinach, oats and seasonings. Form into 18 meat balls. Place in a non-stick roasting tin and cook for 20 minutes.

Mix together the stock, diluted tomato purée, sherry and cornflour, and simmer until thickened. Drain excess fat from the meat and pour the tomato sauce over. Reset the temperature to 180°C/350°F/gas 4 and cook for 30 minutes. Serve with the hot rice.

Chilli con carne

Serves 3
Per serving: 232 KCal, 30.3 g carbohydrate, 16 g protein, 5.2 g fat,
28 mg cholesterol, 10.4 g fibre, 72 mg sodium

115 g/4 oz lean minced beef
65 g/2½ oz onion, chopped
1 clove garlic, crushed
pinch ground cumin

450 g/1 lb tin baked beans
140 g/5 oz tomatoes and green
* chillies*

In a saucepan, brown the beef, stirring to separate, and cook the onion with garlic and cumin until tender. Add the remaining ingredients. Bring to the boil; reduce heat. Simmer uncovered for 10 minutes, stirring occasionally.

Tacos　See photograph, page 98

Serves 6
Per serving: 230 KCal, 17.3 g carbohydrate, 19.6 g protein, 9.2 g fat, 60 mg cholesterol, 2.1 g fibre, 210 mg sodium

450 g/1 lb lean minced beef
1 medium onion, chopped
2 cloves garlic, crushed

10 ml/2 tsp chilli powder
10 ml/2 tsp oregano
1.25 ml/¼ tsp salt

dash of tabasco sauce
2.5 ml/½ tsp ground cumin
115 ml/4 fl oz tinned tomatoes
2.5 ml/½ tsp tomato purée

6 taco shells
½ lettuce, shredded
140 g/5 oz tomatoes, chopped
40 g/1½ oz low-fat cheese, grated

In a large frying pan, brown the minced beef. Add the chopped onion and garlic and cook gently for 5 minutes. Drain off any excess fat. Mix next 7 ingredients together, add to beef and simmer for about 10 minutes. Divide the mixture between the taco shells and top with shredded lettuce, chopped tomatoes and the cheese.

Tijuana pie

Serves 8
Per serving: 457 KCal, 42.4 g carbohydrate, 35 g protein, 16.4 g fat, 69 mg cholesterol, 16.3 g fibre, 234 mg sodium

450 g/1 lb minced beef
1 onion, chopped
1 clove garlic, crushed
1.25 ml/¼ tsp pepper
280 ml/10 fl oz barbecue sauce
225 g/8 oz tinned tomatoes
2.5 ml/½ tsp tomato purée

6 corn tortillas
335 g/12 oz low-fat cheese,
  shredded
900 g/2 lb tinned beans
450 g/1 lb can sweetcorn,
  drained

Brown the beef, onion and garlic in a frying pan. Pour off any excess fat and season with pepper. Mix together the barbecue sauce, tomatoes and purée. Lightly oil a heavy-bottomed pan or a slow cooker. Place a tortilla in the bottom of the pot and spoon some of the meat mixture on to it with a little sauce and cheese. Top with another tortilla and spoon over some beans, cheese and sweetcorn. Continue the layers, finishing with cheese. Cover and cook on low heat for 5–7 hours. Serve with additional hot tortillas.

OVERLEAF: Tacos (*top right*, see page 96), Chicken with peaches (*top left*, see page 100), Oriental chicken with rice (*bottom centre and right*, see page 101)

Meat loaf

Serves 4
Per serving: 236 KCal, 6.7 g carbohydrate, 25.2 g protein, 12.0 g
fat, 84 mg cholesterol, 1.9 g fibre, 171 mg sodium

450 g/1 lb lean minced beef *50 g/2 oz celery, diced*
40 g/1½ oz rolled oats *1.25 ml/¼ tsp pepper*
50 g/2 oz green pepper, chopped *5 ml/1 tsp Worcestershire sauce*
50 g/2 oz onion, chopped *2.5 ml/½ tsp seasoning salt (optional)*

Heat oven to 180°C/350°F/gas 4.
Mix together all the ingredients. Place in a 900 g/2 lb loaf tin.
Bake uncovered for 1 hour.

POULTRY

Chicken with peaches   See photograph, page 98

Serves 6
Per serving: 411 KCal, 39.7 g carbohydrate, 46.1 g protein, 7.5 g
fat, 116 mg cholesterol, 3.5 g fibre, 131 (311) mg sodium*

1 × 1.1 kg–1.4 kg/2½–3 lb chicken *50 ml/2 fl oz soy sauce*
1.25 ml/¼ tsp pepper *1 large onion, sliced*
170 g/6 oz tinned tomatoes *1 green pepper, cut into rings*
5 ml/1 tsp tomato purée *15 g/1 tbsp cornflour*
420 g/15 oz tin sliced peaches in *500 g/1 lb 2 oz cooked hot rice*
light syrup

Heat oven to 230°C/450°F/gas 8.
Cut the chicken into 6 pieces and remove skin. Sprinkle with
pepper and place in an ovenproof dish and cook for 20 minutes.
Pour off any fat. Mix together the tinned tomatoes, purée and
peach syrup. Make up to 575 ml/1 pint with water. Add soy sauce
and pour over chicken. Arrange onion and pepper rings on top.
Cover and cook for 30 minutes.
Mix the cornflour with 50 ml/2 fl oz water and add to chicken
with the peaches. Cover and cook for another 10 minutes. Serve
with the rice.

---

*See note, page 92.

Pollo cacciatore

Serves 6
Per serving: 110 KCal, 3.1 g carbohydrate, 18.2 g protein, 2.7 g fat,
48 mg cholesterol, 1.2 g fibre, 142 mg sodium

50 g/2 oz fresh mushrooms, sliced
280 g/10 oz tomatoes, chopped
1 green pepper, chopped
50 g/2 oz onion, chopped
45 ml/3 tbsp cooking sherry

50 ml/2 fl oz chicken stock
1 clove garlic, crushed
3 chicken breasts, skinned and halved
pinch of pepper
15 ml/1 tsp mixed dried herbs

Mix together all the vegetables in a large frying pan, add the
sherry, stock and garlic. Place the chicken pieces on top of the
vegetables and sprinkle with pepper and herbs. Bring to the boil,
cover and reduce heat. Simmer gently for 25 minutes or until the
chicken is tender.

Oriental chicken   See photograph, page 98

Serves 4
Per serving: 214 KCal, 8.7 g carbohydrate, 22.2 g protein, 10 g fat,
51 mg cholesterol, 2.9 g fibre, 86 (221) mg sodium*

2 whole chicken breasts
30 ml/2 tbsp soy sauce
15 ml/1 tbsp cornflour
75 ml/3 fl oz chicken stock
30 ml/2 tbsp dry sherry
1.25 ml/¼ tsp sugar

1.25 ml/¼ tsp pepper
30 ml/2 tbsp vegetable oil
50 g/2 oz mushrooms, sliced
280 g/10 oz tin bamboo shoots,
* sliced*
170 g/6 oz mangetout peas,

Skin and bone the chicken breasts, thinly slice into bite-sized
pieces. Mix together the soy sauce and cornflour; stir in the chicken
stock, sherry, sugar and pepper. Set aside.
   Heat a large frying pan or wok over a high heat; add the oil. Stir-
fry the mushrooms and bamboo shoots for 1 minute. Remove
with a slotted spoon. Add the mangetouts and stir-fry for 1
minute. Remove. Add more oil if necessary. Stir-fry the chicken
pieces for 2–3 minutes or until cooked. Stir in the reserved stock.
Cook, stirring until thickened. Return all the vegetables to the
frying pan or wok; cover and cook for a further 2 minutes. Serve
with hot cooked rice, if desired.

*See note, page 92.

Cashew chicken

Serves 4
Per serving: 272 KCal, 11.6 g carbohydrate, 14.3 g protein, 18.8 g fat, 22 mg cholesterol, 1.1 g fibre, 32 (167) mg sodium*

15 ml/1 tbsp cornflour dissolved in
  30 ml/2 tbsp soy sauce and
  60 ml/4 tbsp water
2 whole chicken breasts, skinned, boned and cubed
30 ml/2 tbsp oil
1 small onion, cubed
170 g/6 oz green vegetables, cut up (eg,

green beans, broccoli, parboiled green peas or asparagus)
115 g/4 oz cashew nuts
pinch white pepper (optional)

Garnish:
1 spring onion, finely chopped

Pour the cornflour and soy sauce mixture over the chicken and let stand 20 minutes or longer in the refrigerator.

Set a wok or large non-stick frying pan on a high heat. Add 15 ml/1 tbsp of oil and heat. Take the chicken out of the marinade and stir-fry 2–3 minutes, or until white. Remove to a plate and keep warm. Add the remaining oil. Stir-fry the onion for 1 minute, then add the green vegetables. Stir-fry until tender and crisp. Return the chicken to the pan. Stir in the marinade and cook until thickened. Stir in the cashews and season with pepper, if using. Garnish with the spring onion and serve immediately.

Chicken and rice

Serves 6
Per serving: 184 KCal, 22.3 g carbohydrate, 17.1 g protein, 2.9 g fat, 38 mg cholesterol, 2.3 g fibre, 263 mg sodium

5 ml/1 tsp chicken seasoning
3 chicken breasts, skinned and halved
225 g/8 oz long-grain rice

225 ml/8 fl oz chicken stock
30 ml/2 tbsp pimiento, diced
10 ml/2 tsp chopped parsley

Heat oven to 220°C/425°F/gas 7.

Sprinkle the seasoning over the chicken. Place in a shallow casserole and cook for 20 minutes. Pour off any fat. Add the rice, stock, pimiento and parsley. Stir well. Arrange the chicken over the rice mixture. Cover tightly, reduce heat to 180°C/350°F/gas 4 and cook for a further 30 minutes or until the liquid is absorbed and the rice and chicken are tender.

---

*See note ,page 92.

Cashew chicken

Chicken chop suey

Serves 6
Per serving: 359 KCal, 40.4 g carbohydrate, 29.3 g protein, 8.9 g fat, 64 mg cholesterol, 5.9 g fibre, 375 (565) mg sodium*

30 ml/2 tbsp vegetable oil
450 g/ 1 lb chicken breasts, skinned, boned and cut into 5 × 1 cm/2 × ½ in strips
335 g/12 oz onions, sliced
75 g/3 oz mushrooms, sliced
½ green pepper, chopped

1 × 280 g/10 oz tin water chestnuts, sliced
225 g/8 oz frozen Chinese or mixed vegetables
75 ml/3 fl oz soy sauce
30 ml/2 tbsp cornflour
500 g/1 lb 2 oz cooked rice

Heat the oil in a heavy frying pan or wok. Brown the chicken in the hot oil for 2–4 minutes, stirring constantly. Add the onions, mushrooms, green pepper and water chestnuts and cook for 2–4 minutes, stirring. Add the mixed vegetables. Blend the soy sauce and cornflour with 225 ml/8 fl oz water. Pour into the chicken mixture and cook until thickened, stirring constantly. Serve with the hot rice.

Chicken fruit salad

Serves 6
Per serving: 197 KCal, 18.4 g carbohydrate, 23.1 g protein, 3.4 g fat, 60 mg cholesterol, 2.2 g fibre, 98 mg sodium

500 g/1 lb 2 oz cooked chicken, diced
115 g/4 oz celery, chopped
115 g/4 oz seedless grapes, halved

435 g/15½ oz tin pineapple pieces in natural juice
450 g/1 lb satsumas, peeled and segmented
50 ml/2 fl oz low-fat plain yoghurt
lettuce leaves

Toss all the ingredients together, chill and serve on a bed of lettuce.

Turkey-rice sauté

Serves 6
Per serving: 229 KCal, 26.7 g carbohydrate, 17.6 g protein, 5.8 g fat, 40 mg cholesterol, 3.8 g fibre, 385 mg sodium

30 ml/2 tbsp vegetable oil
1 clove garlic, crushed
50 g/2 oz onion, chopped
50 g/2 oz green pepper, chopped
115 g/4 oz celery, sliced
75 g/3 oz carrots, sliced

335 g/12 oz cooked turkey, chopped
500 g/1 lb 2 oz cooked long-grain rice (see page 82)
30 ml/2 tbsp soy sauce
45 ml/3 tbsp orange juice

*See note, page 92.

Heat the oil and garlic in a 30 cm/12 in non-stick frying pan or wok. Add the vegetables to the hot oil and cook, stirring constantly, for 2–4 minutes, until tender but still crisp. Stir in the turkey and rice. Add soy sauce and orange juice and bring to the boil. Pour into a heated serving dish and serve immediately.

MAIN DISH CASSEROLES

Broccoli–ham rollups

Serves 6
Per serving: 134 KCal, 4.7 g carbohydrate, 13.3 g protein, 6.9 g fat, 26 mg cholesterol, 1.3 g fibre, 309 mg sodium

170 g/6 oz frozen broccoli spears   *5 ml/1 tsp Dijon mustard*
15 g/½ oz margarine   *75 g/3 oz low-fat cheese, shredded*
25 g/1 oz wholemeal flour   *170 g/6 oz cooked ham (6 slices)*
225 ml/8 fl oz skimmed milk   *paprika pepper*

Heat oven to 180°C/350°F/gas 4.
Cook broccoli until just tender. Melt the margarine, stir in the flour and cook over a low heat for 1–2 minutes, then gradually pour in the warmed milk, stirring constantly. Add the mustard and cheese once the sauce has thickened, and stir until the cheese has melted. Roll the broccoli in the ham slices and place in an oven-proof baking dish. Pour the sauce over the ham rolls and sprinkle with paprika pepper. Cook for 20 minutes.

Beef and rice dinner

Serves 6
Per serving: 150 KCal, 17.7 g carbohydrate, 10.1 g protein, 4.3 g fat, 28 mg cholesterol, 2.4 g fibre, 187 mg sodium

335 g/12 oz cooked brown rice (see   *1 small onion, chopped*
page 82)   *½ green pepper, chopped*
2.5 ml/½ tsp seasoning salt   *1 clove garlic, crushed*
225 g/8 oz lean minced beef   *2.5 ml/½ tsp mixed dried herbs*
225 ml/8 fl oz tomato juice

Season the rice with the seasoning salt. Brown the minced beef and drain off any excess fat. Simmer together the tomato juice, onion, pepper and garlic for 8–10 minutes, then add the beef, rice and herbs. Simmer for 10 minutes, stirring occasionally.

Cheesy garden casserole

Serves 6
Per serving: 254 KCal, 32.9 g carbohydrate, 15.2 g protein, 6.8 g fat, 22 mg cholesterol, 5.2 g fibre, 51 mg sodium

115 g/4 oz broccoli, chopped
115 g/4 oz cauliflower florets
115 g/4 oz carrots, sliced
115 g/4 oz courgettes, sliced
115 g/4 oz green beans, cut into
  2.5 cm/1 in pieces
335 g/12 oz cooked brown rice (see
  page 82)
freshly ground black pepper
5 ml/1 tsp oregano
450 g/16 oz tinned tomatoes
115 g/4 oz low-fat cheese, grated

Heat oven to 190°C/375°F/gas 5.
  Cook the vegetables in boiling water until just tender, about 5–7 minutes, and drain. Place the rice in an ovenproof dish, spoon the drained vegetables on top and sprinkle over the pepper and oregano. Pour over the tomatoes. Bake for 30 minutes. Sprinkle the cheese over the casserole and return to the oven for about 5 minutes, or until cheese has melted.

Vegetarian pasticcio

Serves 2
Per serving: 173 KCal, 22.4 g carbohydrate, 15.3 g protein, 2.5 g fat, 0 mg cholesterol, 4.4 g fibre, 385 mg sodium

2 medium courgettes, coarsely grated
salt
2 large egg whites, lightly beaten
50 g/2 oz low-fat cheese
30 ml/2 tbsp flour
1.25 ml/¼ tsp dried basil
pinch of pepper
115 g/4 oz tinned tomatoes
5 ml/1 tsp tomato purée
25 g/1 oz mushrooms, sliced
15 ml/1 tbsp onion, chopped
1.25 ml/¼ tsp dried oregano

Place the courgettes in a colander, sprinkle lightly with salt and let stand 30 minutes.
  Heat oven to 180°C/350°F/gas 4. Rinse the courgettes and dry thoroughly. Combine the courgettes with egg whites, 40 g/1½ oz cheese, the flour, basil and pepper. Spread the mixture on to a lightly oiled 25 cm/10 in quiche dish or baking tin, or a 28 ×

18 cm/11 × 7 in dish. Bake for 20 minutes, or until firm. Place under the grill for 3 minutes. Top evenly with the tomatoes mixed to a sauce with the purée, then the remaining low-fat cheese, mushrooms, onion and oregano. Return to the oven for about 5 minutes at 180°C/350°F/gas 4, or until the cheese has melted.

Golden pilaff

Serves 4
Per serving: 210 KCal, 21.0 g carbohydrate, 8 g protein, 10.4 g fat, 0 mg cholesterol, 6.9 g fibre, 332 mg sodium

40 g/1½ oz margarine   *115 g/4 oz rolled oats*
25 g/1 oz mushrooms, chopped   *225 ml/8 fl oz chicken stock*
75 g/3 oz green pepper, chopped   *25 g/1 oz oat bran cereal*
50 g/2 oz spring onions, sliced

In a medium frying pan, melt the margarine. Sauté the mushrooms, green pepper and onion for 2–3 minutes. Add the oats and cook over a medium heat until they are lightly browned. Add the stock and continue cooking for 2–3 minutes. Stir in the oat bran cereal; continue cooking until liquid has evaporated, about 1–2 minutes.

Sweetcorn casserole

Serves 6
Per serving: 124 KCal, 14.1 g carbohydrate, 6.7 g protein, 4.4 g fat, 1 mg cholesterol, 4.3 g fibre, 387 mg sodium

170 g/6 oz cottage cheese   *1.25 ml/¼ tsp dry mustard*
25 g/1 oz margarine, melted   *15 ml/1 tbsp pimiento*
5 ml/1 tsp flour   *5 ml/1 tsp dried parsley*
5 ml/1 tsp chicken stock   *450 g/1 lb sweetcorn kernels*

Heat oven to 180°C/350°F/gas 4.
Sieve the cottage cheese. Beat in the margarine and flour. Gradually stir in the remaining ingredients. Pour into an ovenproof dish. Bake for 25–30 minutes.

Macaroni casserole

Serves 6
Per serving: 280 KCal, 21.9 g carbohydrate, 19.7 g protein, 12.6 g fat, 43 mg cholesterol, 1.7 g fibre, 180 mg sodium

225 g/8 oz macaroni   *335 g/12 oz minced beef*
65 g/2½ oz low-fat cheese, grated   *30 ml/2 tbsp green pepper*

➡

115 g/4 oz onion, chopped   *pinch of pepper*
225 g/8 oz tin Italian tomatoes   *25 g/1 oz margarine*
10 ml/2 tsp tomato purée   *40 g/1½ oz wholemeal flour*
5 ml/1 tsp oregano   *250 ml/9 fl oz skimmed milk*

Heat oven to 180°C/350°F/gas 4.

Cook the macaroni according to packet instructions; drain. Immediately stir in 40 g/1½ oz cheese. Set aside.

In a large saucepan cook the minced beef, green pepper and onion until the meat is lightly browned. Drain off any excess fat. Stir in the tomatoes and purée, oregano and a pinch of pepper. Set aside.

Melt the margarine and add the flour. Stir in the milk. Bring to the boil, simmer until the mixture begins to thicken.

Layer half of the macaroni mixture in an ovenproof dish, add half of the meat mixture and repeat layers. Bake for 40 minutes. Add the remaining cheese and cook for a further 5 minutes to melt the cheese.

Lasagne

Serves 6
Per serving: 351 KCal, 42 g carbohydrate, 25.3 g protein, 9.1 g fat, 40 mg cholesterol, 7.1 g fibre, 345 mg sodium

225 g/8 oz lean minced beef   *170 g/6 oz tomato purée*
1 large onion, chopped   *25 g/1 oz chopped parsley*
1 clove garlic, crushed   *5 ml/1 tsp oregano*
1 medium green pepper, chopped   *10 ml/2 tsp basil*
2 medium courgettes, chopped   *6 sheets lasagne, cooked*
1 stick celery, chopped   *170 g/6 oz cottage cheese*
1 × 780 g/1 lb 12 oz tin whole   *115 g/4 oz mozzarella cheese, sliced*
tomatoes, chopped

Heat oven to 180°C/350°F/gas 4.

In a large saucepan brown the minced beef, onion, garlic and green pepper. Drain off any excess fat. Add the courgettes, celery, tomatoes, tomato purée, parsley, oregano and basil and bring to the boil. Cover, reduce heat and simmer for 30 minutes. Uncover and cook until sauce has thickened.

In a lightly oiled 24 × 30.5 cm/9½ × 12 in ovenproof dish layer the lasagne, sauce, cottage cheese and mozzarella cheese. Finish with a layer of mozzarella. Cook for 30–40 minutes, until lightly browned.

Parmigiana

Serves 6
Per serving: 208 KCal, 18.8 g carbohydrate, 14.5 g protein, 8.3 g fat, 22 mg cholesterol, 4.1 g fibre, 39 mg sodium

1 whole aubergine (about 450 g/1 lb)
1 large egg white, lightly beaten
50 g/2 oz rolled oats
2 medium tomatoes, sliced

225 g/8 oz mozzarella cheese, sliced
10 ml/2 tsp tomato purée
1.25 ml/¼ tsp basil
225 g/8 oz tinned tomatoes, sieved

Heat oven to 230°C/450°F/gas 8.

Slice the aubergine into 1 cm/½ in rounds. Dip into egg white and then into the oats. Place in a 25 cm/10 in ovenproof dish and bake for 15 minutes. Arrange tomato slices and mozzarella cheese on top of the baked aubergine. Stir the purée and basil into the tinned tomatoes and pour over. Bake for another 15–20 minutes.

Tostadas

Makes 8
Per serving: 179 KCal, 26.5 g carbohydrate, 8 g protein, 4.6 g fat, 0 mg cholesterol, 7 g fibre, 178 mg sodium

450 g/1 lb tin baked beans
140 g/5 oz cooked kidney beans (see
*   page 76)*
25 g/1 oz margarine
50 g/2 oz onion, chopped
10 ml/2 tsp chilli powder

30 ml/2 tbsp taco sauce
8 tostada or taco shells
shredded lettuce
diced tomatoes
50 g/2 oz low-fat cheese, grated

In a bowl, mash the beans. In a frying pan, melt the margarine and cook the onion with the chilli powder until tender. Add the beans and taco sauce. Cook for 5 minutes, stirring frequently.

Divide the bean mixture between the shells. Top with remaining ingredients.

Spaghetti with mushroom sauce

Serves 4
Per serving: 132 KCal, 18.7 g carbohydrate, 4.4 g protein, 4.4 g fat, 0 mg cholesterol, 4.6 g fibre, 193 mg sodium

2 medium onions, chopped
1 clove garlic, chopped
15 ml/1 tbsp oil
1 green pepper, chopped
450 g/1 lb tin tomatoes
115 g/4 oz tomato purée
5 ml/1 tsp dried basil
10 ml/2 tsp cumin
2.5 ml/½ tsp freshly ground pepper

10 ml/2 tsp artificial sweetener
*   (optional)*
5 ml/1 tsp Worcestershire sauce
3 bay leaves
115 g/4 oz mushrooms, sliced or
*   2 × 115 g/4 oz tins mushrooms,*
*   drained*
115 g/4 oz wholemeal spaghetti

In a frying pan soften the onion and garlic in oil, then add the green pepper and cook together until the vegetables are tender. Mix the tomatoes and purée with all the other seasonings and flavourings except the bay leaves. Stir well and add to the frying pan. Then add the bay leaves. Simmer for 30 minutes, adding the mushrooms 10 minutes before the end of cooking. Thin down sauce with a little water if necessary. Remove the bay leaves.

Cook the spaghetti according to the packet instructions. Serve very hot with the sauce on top.

FRUIT AND DESSERTS

We usually have fresh fruit for dessert – apples, peaches, pears grapes, oranges, pineapple – or make a salad of different fruits, diced and topped with shredded coconut and a few chopped nuts. For variety I provide suggestions for different fruit-based desserts. We usually use artificial sweetener to reduce the calorie content but you can substitute other sweeteners of your choice, as suggested under Using the HCF diet.

Gingered fruit salad

Serves 4
Per serving: 84 KCal, 17.7 g carbohydrate, 2.2 g protein, 0.5 g fat, 0 mg cholesterol, 3.2 g fibre, 32 mg sodium

2 medium apples, cored, sliced and sprinkled with a little lemon juice to prevent discoloration
2 medium oranges, pared and segmented
lettuce
115 ml/4 fl oz low-fat lemon yoghurt
10 ml/2 tsp preserved ginger, finely chopped

Arrange the apple slices and orange segments on four lettuce-lined plates. Combine the yoghurt and ginger; place a little yoghurt mixture on each salad.

Gingered fruit salad (*top*), Strawberry-banana freeze (*centre*, see page 114), Frozen fresh fruit salad (*bottom*, see page 112)

Fresh fruit salad

Serves 8
Per serving: 62 KCal, 13.8 g carbohydrate, 1.3 g protein, 0.2 fat,
0 mg cholesterol, 1.9 g fibre, 9 mg sodium

3 peaches
1 melon
170 g/6 oz water melon

170 g/6 oz blackberries, strawberries
or other fresh berries
75 ml/3 fl oz frozen orange juice
concentrate

Peel the peaches and cut into 1 cm/½ in pieces. Halve the melon,
remove seeds and cut into 1.5 cm/¾ in cubes. Mix all the fruit
together and chill. Stir in the orange juice concentrate before
serving.

Frozen fresh fruit salad

Serves 8   See photograph, page 110
Per serving: 102 KCal, 10.1 g carbohydrate, 4.8 g protein, 4.7 g fat,
1 mg cholesterol, 1.2 g fibre, 180 mg sodium

335 g/12 oz fresh fruit: peaches,
nectarines, strawberries, bananas or
seedless grapes; use one kind or a
combination
artificial sweetener to taste
450 ml/16 fl oz low-fat plain
yoghurt

5 ml/1 tsp powdered ginger
30 ml/2 tbsp lemon juice
50 g/2 oz chopped nuts (optional)
additional fresh fruit to decorate

Set refrigerator control at lowest point.
    Peel and dice the fruit you have chosen; sprinkle with just
enough artificial sweetener to sweeten slightly. Cover and leave to
marinate. Beat together the yoghurt, ginger and lemon juice. Fold
in the fruit. Add the nuts, if using. Pour mixture into a lightly oiled
mould, ice cube trays, or into small, individual moulds, and freeze
for about 3 hours. When firm, remove from the moulds by dipping
them, almost to the top, in hot water for a few seconds, then invert
on to a plate. Serve the frozen salad decorated with additional
fruit.

Tropical fruit salad

Serves 4
Per serving: 82 KCal, 15.9 g carbohydrate, 1.0 g protein, 1.6 g fat,
0 mg cholesterol, 2.4 g fibre, 2 mg sodium

4 fresh apricots, stoned and diced
1 banana, sliced
10 ml/2 tsp lemon juice

30 ml/2 tbsp unsweetened coconut
170 g/6 oz fresh pineapple, peeled
 and diced

Toss all the ingredients together and serve.

Orange and apple sauce salad

Serves 4
Per serving: 136 KCal, 31.2 g carbohydrate, 2.3 g protein, 0.2 g fat,
0 mg cholesterol, 2.1 g fibre, 69 mg sodium

75 g/3 oz packet orange-flavoured
 gelatine (eg, QuickJel)

225 g/8 oz apple sauce
1 apple, cored and diced

In a bowl dissolve the gelatine in 225 ml/8 fl oz hot water. Stir in
apple sauce, diced apple and 115 ml/4 fl oz cold water. Pour mixture into 4 small bowls. Chill until set.

Fruit cup

Serves 6
Per serving: 102 KCal, 20.3 g carbohydrate, 1.1 g protein, 1.8 g fat,
0 mg cholesterol, 2.6 g fibre, 2 mg sodium

45 ml/3 tbsp frozen orange juice
 concentrate
1 medium apple, cored and chopped
1 medium orange, peeled, segmented
 and chopped

1 medium peach, stoned and chopped
1 medium banana, peeled and sliced
50 g/2 oz seedless grapes, halved
50 g/2 oz blackberries
30 ml/2 tbsp walnuts, finely chopped

Place the orange concentrate in a large bowl and mix lightly with
the fruits. Cover and chill. Sprinkle each serving with chopped
walnuts.

NB Skins of apple and peach may be removed, if desired.

Hot fruit compote

Serves 6
Per serving: 143 KCal, 29.9 g carbohydrate, 1.2 g protein, 2.1 g fat,
0 mg cholesterol, 3.8 g fibre, 31 mg sodium

➡

1 × 420 g/15 oz tin Victoria plums,   *1 × 300 g/11 oz tin mandarin*
drained   *pieces*
1 × 420 g/15 oz tin peach halves,   *15 ml/1 tbsp demerara sugar*
drained   *2.5 ml/½ tsp grated lemon rind*
                                         15 ml/1 tbsp margarine, melted

Heat oven to 220°C/425°F/gas 7.
Place the plums and peach halves in alternate layers in a baking
dish. Drain the mandarin pieces and reserve the liquid. Arrange
the mandarin pieces over the fruit in the baking dish. Mix
together the mandarin liquid, demerara sugar, lemon rind and
margarine. Pour over the fruit. Bake for 10–15 minutes.

Strawberry–banana freeze

Serves 8   See photograph, page 110
Per serving: 58 KCal, 10.7 g carbohydrate, 3.1 g protein, 0.3 g fat,
1 mg cholesterol, 1.3 g fibre, 107 mg sodium

450 g/1 lb strawberries, hulled   *30 ml/2 tbsp calorie-reduced straw-*
1 medium size ripe banana, sliced   *berry jam*
                                        225 ml/8 fl oz low-fat plain yoghurt

Set the refrigerator at the lowest temperature – or use the deep-
freeze.
Reserve 3 strawberries for decoration. Purée the remaining
strawberries and banana in blender goblet or liquidizer. Add the
jam and yoghurt; purée again until blended. Pour the mixture
into ice cream trays and freeze about 2 hours, or until firm around
the edges. Pour into a large bowl and beat well until light and
fluffy. Return to the ice cream trays and freeze 1–2 hours, or until
firm. To serve, turn into a dish and decorate with sliced
strawberries.

Peachy fruit dessert

Serves 5
Per serving: 99 KCal, 23.4 g carbohydrate, 1.0 g protein, 0.2 g fat,
0 mg cholesterol, 2.9 g fibre, 6 mg sodium

420 g/15 oz tin peach halves in   *2.5 ml/½ tsp vanilla essence*
natural juice   *170 g/6 oz cubed melon flesh*
5 ml/1 tsp cornflour   *140 g/5 oz fresh strawberries, hulled*
1.25 ml/¼ tsp cinnamon   *½ small banana, thickly sliced*
2.5 ml/½ tsp allspice   *1 small apple, cut into wedges*

In a blender goblet or food processor place the undrained
peaches, cornflour, cinnamon and allspice; blend until nearly
smooth. Pour into a small saucepan; bring slowly to the boil, stirring constantly. Remove from heat; stir in vanilla essence and
leave to cool. Arrange the remaining fruit in individual serving dishes
and spoon the peach sauce over.

Spiced peaches

Serves 4
Per serving: 40 KCal, 9.2 g carbohydrate, 0.5 g protein, 0.1 g fat,
0 mg cholesterol, 1.7 g fibre, 3 mg sodium

420 g/15 oz tin peach halves in   *1 × 15 cm/6 in cinnamon stick*
natural juice   *3 whole cloves*

Pour the peaches with their juice into a saucepan (liquid should
cover the fruit). Add the cinnamon stick and cloves. Bring to the
boil. Reduce heat and simmer for 10 minutes.
   Serve 2 halves per person hot as a pudding, or chill and use as an
accompaniment to cold meats.

Hot orange sauce   See photograph, page 37

Serves 16
Per serving: 29 KCal, 3.4 g carbohydrate, 0.3 g protein, 1.6 g fat,
0 mg cholesterol, 0.3 g fibre, 10 g sodium

15 ml/1 tbsp margarine   *1 large fresh orange, peeled and*
15 ml/1 tbsp vegetable oil   *chopped*
30 ml/2 tbsp wholemeal flour   *pinch of mace*
225 ml/8 fl oz orange juice

Melt the margarine and oil in a saucepan. Mix in the flour, stirring
over medium heat for 2 minutes. Stir in the orange juice and bring
to the boil. Simmer until thick and creamy. Remove from heat
and let cool. Stir in fresh orange and mace. Serve over crêpes
or waffles.

Peach crumble

Serves 6
Per serving: 79 KCal, 11.5 g carbohydrate, 1.3 g protein, 3.1 g fat,
0 mg cholesterol, 2.3 g fibre, 64 mg sodium

700 g/1½ lb fresh peaches, sliced or   *15 ml/1 tbsp artificial sweetener*
2 × 450 g/1 lb tins sliced peaches,   *2.5 ml/½ tsp cinnamon*
drained   *pinch nutmeg*
                                         pinch salt
Topping: *25 ml/1½ tbsp margarine*
25 g/1 oz flour   *15 g/½ oz rolled oats*

Heat oven to 200°C/400°F/gas 6.
   In a shallow ovenproof dish combine the fresh peaches with
75 ml/3 fl oz water, *or* pour in the tinned peaches. In a small bowl
rub together all the ingredients for the topping. Sprinkle over the
peaches. Bake for 40 minutes or until lightly browned. Serve
warm.

Pears with melba sauce

Serves 4
Per serving: 93 KCal, 21.7 g carbohydrate, 0.8 g protein, 0.3 g fat,
0 mg cholesterol, 4.3 g fibre, 2 mg sodium

140 g/5 oz fresh or frozen raspberries   420 g/15 oz tin pear halves, drained
5 ml/1 tsp granulated sugar

Put the raspberries, 75 ml/3 fl oz water and the sugar into a blender
goblet or food processor. Purée for 30–60 seconds at high speed,
until smooth. Serve over the pear halves.

Banana split

Serves 2
Per serving: 289 KCal, 20.1 g carbohydrate, 8.4 g protein, 19.4 g
fat, 1 mg cholesterol, 3.3 g fibre, 2 mg sodium

1 banana   *6 walnuts, chopped*
115 ml/4 fl oz low-fat plain yoghurt   nutmeg to taste

Split the banana, top with yoghurt, nuts and nutmeg. Share
with someone!

Apple crumble

Serves 4
Per serving: 144 KCal, 19.1 g carbohydrate, 3.3 g protein, 6 g fat,
0 mg cholesterol, 5.7 g fibre, 40 mg sodium

770 g/1 lb 12 oz apple, peeled and   Topping:
  sliced   *40 g/1½ oz oat bran cereal* or
20 ml/4 tsp artificial sweetener   *rolled oats*
10 ml/2 tsp lemon juice   *30 ml/2 tbsp chopped walnuts*
2.5 ml/½ tsp ground cinnamon   *5 ml/1 tsp artificial sweetener*
                                       15 ml/1 tbsp polyunsaturated
                                         margarine, melted

Combine all the ingredients for the fruit layer; add 50 ml/2 fl oz
water and toss together lightly. Put in an ungreased 20 cm/8 in
square ovenproof dish.
  For the topping: heat oven to 190°C/375°F/gas 5. In a small
bowl, combine the oat bran cereal, nuts and artificial sweetener.
Add the margarine and mix well. Sprinkle over the apples. Bake
for about 30 minutes or until the apples are tender and the topping is lightly browned. Serve warm or chilled.

Baked apple

Serves 1
Per serving: 106 KCal, 20.7 g carbohydrate, 0.8 g protein, 2.2 g fat,
0 mg cholesterol, 4.0 g fibre, 2 mg sodium

1 large cooking apple   *5 ml/1 tsp nuts, chopped*
5 ml/1 tsp raisins   *pinch of cinnamon*
5 ml/1 tsp dried dates or figs, chopped

Heat oven to 200°C/400°F/gas 6.
    Wash the apple. Core, leaving 0.5 cm/¼ in at the bottom to hold the filling. In a mixing bowl, combine the raisins, dates and nuts. Fill the apple centre with the mixture. Sprinkle with cinnamon. Wrap the apple in foil. Place in a shallow baking dish and add 30 ml/2 tbsp water. Bake for about 30 minutes or until soft.

Apple bundt cake

Serves 12
Per serving: 225 KCal, 48.5 g carbohydrate, 5.8 g protein, 0.9 g fat,
0 mg cholesterol, 3.8 g fibre, 135 mg sodium

170 g/6 oz dried apples   *10 ml/2 tsp ground cinnamon*
115 ml/4 fl oz apple juice   *1.25 ml/¼ tsp grated nutmeg*
40 g/1½ oz raisins   *1.25 ml/¼ tsp ground allspice*
115 g/4 oz plain flour   *4 egg whites*
115 g/4 oz wholemeal flour   *5 ml/1 tsp vanilla essence*
10 ml/2 tsp baking powder   *170 g/6 oz Grapenuts cereal*
10 ml/2 tsp bicarbonate of soda

Heat oven to 170°C/325°F/gas 3.
    Combine the dried apples, apple juice, 115 ml/4 fl oz water and the raisins in a bowl. Cover with clingfilm and store in the refrigerator for 4–6 hours.
    Sift the flours, baking powder, bicarbonate of soda, cinnamon, nutmeg and allspice into a large bowl. Whisk the egg whites until soft peaks form. Fold into the flour mixture. Add the apple–raisin mixture, with the vanilla essence and cereal. Stir well. Pour into a non-stick round cake tin. Bake for approximately 1½ hours. Turn the cake out on to a large sheet of foil. Wrap completely and leave for several hours before using.

Crunchy bananas

Serves 6
Per serving: 105 KCal, 19.8 g carbohydrate, 1.3 g protein, 2.3 g fat,
0 mg cholesterol, 2.1 g fibre, 28 mg sodium   ➤

3 bananas	*15 g/½ oz rolled oats*
5 ml/1 tsp lemon juice	*1.25 ml/¼ tsp ground cinnamon*
25 g/1 oz demerara sugar	*1.25 ml/¼ tsp grated nutmeg*
30 ml/2 tbsp wholemeal flour	*15 ml/1 tbsp margarine*

Heat oven to 190°C/375°F/gas 5.

Peel the bananas, cut in half lengthwise and cut each half into two pieces. Place in an ovenproof dish. Sprinkle with lemon juice. In a small bowl mix together the sugar, flour, oats, cinnamon and nutmeg. Rub in the margarine until crumbly. Sprinkle over the bananas. Bake for 15–20 minutes. Serve immediately.

Creamy rice pudding

Serves 4

Per serving: 193 KCal, 31.2 g carbohydrate, 6.4 g protein, 4.7 g fat, 2 mg cholesterol, 0.8 g fibre, 121 mg sodium

335 g/12 oz cooked rice	*pinch of salt*
450 ml/16 fl oz skimmed milk	*25 g/1 oz margarine*
5 ml/1 tsp artificial sweetener	*2.5 ml/½ tsp vanilla essence*

In a small saucepan mix together the rice, milk, artificial sweetener, salt and margarine. Stir over a medium heat until thickened, about 20 minutes. Add the vanilla essence. Serve hot or cold.

ACKNOWLEDGEMENTS

The author acknowledges the help of Gay Anderson for typing
the manuscript, Ruth Duncan and Linda Story.

Lexington, 1984   *J. W. A.*

The publishers would like to thank Morning Foods Ltd, Crewe,
for their help in the preparation of this book.
   The photographs were taken by Paul Williams, assisted by JJ
Crofton; styling by Penny Markham and food preparation by Lisa
Collard.

INDEX

Figures in *italics* refer to illustrations.

Other titles in the series

DIABETES
A practical guide to healthy living
Dr Jim Anderson

THE DIABETICS' DIET BOOK
A new high-fibre eating programme
Dr Jim Mann and the Oxford Dietetic Group

THE DIABETICS' GET FIT BOOK
The complete home workout
Jacki Winter
Introduction by
Dr Barbara Boucher

HIGH BLOOD PRESSURE
What it means for you, and how to control it
Dr Eoin O'Brien and
Prof Kevin O'Malley

BEAT HEART DISEASE
A cardiologist explains how you can help your heart and enjoy a healthier life
Prof Risteard Mulcahy

DON'T FORGET FIBRE IN YOUR DIET
To help avoid many of our commonest diseases
Dr Denis Burkitt

THE HIGH FIBRE COOKBOOK
Recipes for good health
Pamela Westland
Introduced by Denis Burkitt

OVERCOMING ARTHRITIS
A guide to coping with stiff or aching joints
Dr Frank Dudley Hart

THE SALT-FREE DIET BOOK
An appetizing way to help reduce high blood pressure
Dr Graham MacGregor

THE DIABETICS' COOKBOOK
Delicious new recipes for entertaining and all the family
Roberta Longstaff, SRD,
and Dr Jim Mann

VARICOSE VEINS
How they are treated, and what you can do to help
Prof Harold Ellis

ECZEMA AND DERMATITIS
How to cope with inflamed skin
Prof Rona MacKie

ANXIETY AND DEPRESSION
A practical guide to recovery
Prof Robert Priest

ACNE
Advice on clearing your skin
Prof Ronald Marks

OVERCOMING DYSLEXIA
A straightforward guide for families and teachers
Dr Bevé Hornsby

EYES
Their problems and treatments
Michael Glasspool, FRCS

CONQUERING PAIN
How to overcome the discomfort of arthritis, backache, migraine, heart disease, childbirth, period pains and many other common conditions
Dr Sampson Lipton